Ad
Driven: A Fie

In *Driven*, Bill Ireland has given anyone struggling in a challenging situation, wondering where God is and whether anything makes sense anymore, a great gift. In prose that's clear and compelling, Bill shares what he learned in the wilderness: that, there, faith is challenged, prayer is transformed, and all the old religious clichés crack under pressure. By pulling back the curtain on his own struggles following a painful job loss, Bill shows us that, even when the way forward seems murky at best, God can still be trusted—though learning to trust will take all we've got. And it's worth it.

—*L. Roger Owens*
Professor of Christian Spirituality and Ministry
Pittsburgh Theological Seminary

Call it "wilderness" or "the dark night of the soul." Call it "forty days of desert" or "pregnant pause" or "threshold." Whatever the name, this is tough stuff. Most of us hit these walls and hold a public face—a thin facade of "everything is great." Sometimes, however, we are gifted with "honor, hope and generosity" when honesty wins and the authentic self shows up without any makeup.

Ireland, shed of the external armor of thin success and upward professional ascendancy, shows us the anatomy of these moments—up close. And we are gifted with his honest testimony of integrity and grit, of sorrow and disappointment and his gifted way of writing about them. He is real. And in reading this, we too can become real.

—*Linda McKinnish Bridges*
Former Founding Faculty and President
Baptist Theological Seminary at Richmond

All of us will find ourselves in the wilderness at one time or another and Bill Ireland's *Driven* is indispensable for those times. Drawing from his own experience, Bill reminds us that we have reliable guides such as Scripture, spiritual practices, and friendships that will sustain us in those barren, difficult places that are part of life's journey.

—Mona West
Director of Adult Christian Formation
St. David's Episcopal Church
Austin, Texas
Contributing editor of The Queer Bible Commentary

Although Dr. Ireland's wilderness sojourn is personal and therefore unique, he touches on common themes we all confront—to lose and search, to find and renew. His transparency is refreshing and therefore his encouragement to the reader is authentic. By engaging biblical texts as well as including poems and reflections from other writers and thinkers, Ireland helpfully reminds us that there are other guides along the wilderness journey. With pastoral sensitivity and scholarly pragmatism, Ireland offers hope that there is peace on the other side of the wilderness.

—C. Gregory DeLoach
Dean, Mercer University McAfee School of Theology
Atlanta, Georgia

DRIVEN

Smyth & Helwys Publishing, Inc.
6316 Peake Road
Macon, Georgia 31210-3960
1-800-747-3016
©2021 by Bill Ireland
All rights reserved.

Library of Congress Cataloging-in-Publication Data

Names: Ireland, Bill, author.
Title: Driven : a field guide to the wilderness / by Bill Ireland.
Description: First. | Macon, GA : Smyth & Helwys Publishing, 2021. | Includes bibliographical references.
Identifiers: LCCN 2021019158 | ISBN 9781641733090 (paperback)
Subjects: LCSH: Ireland, Bill. | Ex-clergy--Biography. | Wilderness (Theology) | Hidden God. | Faith.
Classification: LCC BV672.5 .I74 2021 | DDC 286.092 [B]--dc23
LC record available at https://lccn.loc.gov/2021019158

Disclaimer of Liability: With respect to statements of opinion or fact available in this work of nonfiction, Smyth & Helwys Publishing Inc. nor any of its employees, makes any warranty, express or implied, or assumes any legal liability or responsibility for the accuracy or completeness of any information disclosed, or represents that its use would not infringe privately owned rights.

DRIVEN

A
FIELD GUIDE
TO THE
WILDERNESS

BILL IRELAND

ALSO BY BILL IRELAND

Daniel: Keeping Faith When the Heat Is On

Preaching the Word: Philippians and Philemon, Colossians

*To Ginny and Mary Virginia,
who shared this journey with me and
loved me all the way through*

CONTENTS

Prologue — xi

Chapter 1: Driven — 1

Chapter 2: Wandering — 15

Chapter 3: Thirsting — 25

Chapter 4: Sustained — 73

Chapter 5: Lessons — 93

Epilogue — 115

Notes — 119

PROLOGUE

This story is intensely personal. In the following pages, I will offer a chronicle of my journey into the wilderness—a journey prompted by my decision to walk away from my last pastorate. It would be a monumental understatement to say that this has been the most difficult chapter of my life. I have learned firsthand what the words "wilderness" and "exile" mean. Nevertheless, my foray into a barren region has not been without its rewards. The wilderness has a lot to teach us, and in my case, I had a lot to learn.

In this brief account, I attempt to describe some of the topography of my journey—the hard features of the wilderness terrain—and also to capture what the wilderness feels like. I will relate some of the discoveries I made along the way and call attention to how barren places sift what we think and believe. In this regard, this story ultimately recounts a journey into my own soul. I relived the rawness of many events that led to my decision to walk away as I reviewed journal entries from 2015–2020. The gifts of time and distance, however, have granted me the complementary gift of perspective. I see things more clearly than I did at the outset. Nevertheless, putting this experience into words has been a source of healing for me, and I wish to extend that grace to others. I have written in hopes of encouraging ministers who have walked the same path I have walked or suspect they may enter the wilderness themselves. As well, I hope to offer something redemptive to those who are not clergy but are also forced to make their way through barren places. No matter who or what we are, we eventually wind up in harsh places. My hope is that what I learned in the wilderness may offer a field guide for those who walk a similar path.

This narrative will not unfold chronologically but thematically. At times I will recount certain events more than once. I do so not because I want to brood over what happened or bore the reader. Instead, I wish to set certain features of my experience in context. Recounting my story in this fashion allows me to describe some of the same experiences from varying perspectives. Where we stand determines what we see. As well, a thematic approach mirrors the way we live. Life does not unfold in a straight line. Instead, we start, stop, zigzag, and often wind up at dead ends. The challenge is to keep walking when the terrain is unvarying and there seems to be no way out.

Thankfully, I have not made this trip alone. Many knew of my experience and encouraged me to get it on paper. Tim Owings, Stephen Cook, and Mary Carol Miller read the early drafts and offered many helpful suggestions for both clarity and style. Keith Gammons, publisher at Smyth & Helwys, took my idea for this book seriously and gave me the go-ahead to write for publication. Leslie Andres gave my work a careful and thorough reading. Her suggestions were spot-on, and I incorporated many of them into the final draft. While I am most grateful for the input of all these readers, I am responsible for any errors or omissions.

I made it to the place where I could write about my experience because I was surrounded by caring friends and a strong family. Allow me to name a few. Mike O'Neill came alongside me during some of the most difficult days when the wilderness was just over the horizon. Julie Johnson, my spiritual director, tended to my struggles and faithfully prayed me through many dark nights of the soul. My leadership coach, Larry McSwain, provided unerring guidance as I weighed the decision to step away. His wisdom and insight were invaluable. As I mention in chapter 4, I was sustained by strong friendships and welcoming communities. I owe them all more than I could ever repay in multiple lifetimes.

Family looms large in my story. My sister, Ellen Hamby, and I have always been close. She and her husband, John, never failed to offer encouragement and support. Laughter has never been a stranger whenever we're together, and our shared zaniness often keeps things in perspective. Their home has truly been a haven of blessing and peace. Most important, I am tremendously grateful for my bride, Ginny Ireland, and our daughter, Mary Virginia. Ginny has long been my lover, my best friend, and my soul mate. Although the last several years have been tough, the experience has deepened our bond. Mary Virginia at times offered wisdom and insight beyond her years. These two never ceased to believe in me, and they both supported me wholeheartedly throughout this long, tortuous journey. Because I could not have made it without them, I dedicate this work to "my girls" as a small token of my abundant love and infinite gratitude.

Now let's get started.

CHAPTER 1

DRIVEN

And the Spirit immediately drove him out into the wilderness.
—Mark 1:12

Before you tell your life what you intend to do with it, listen for what it intends to do with you.
—Parker J. Palmer[1]

By almost every measure, I was a successful pastor. In terms of my education, I had checked all the right boxes and had climbed to the top of the ladder: BA in religion from Mississippi College, MDiv and PhD from Southern Seminary. Following the completion of my studies, I had the privilege of serving some fine churches and had a strong record of achievement. These accomplishments opened the door to extensive service beyond the local congregation. At various junctures, I served on denominational councils and the boards of a hospital and a university. Writing has always been a rewarding and enjoyable component of my ministry, and over time I had compiled an extensive resume of writing for publication—everything from local newspaper articles to books. By and large I had done quite well and was proud of my accomplishments.

Nevertheless, all was not well with my soul. Around my mid-fifties, I sensed something going on beneath the surface of my life. Something was stirring in me that generated a persistent restlessness.

This restlessness showed up in a number of ways. For one, I was increasingly troubled by the way church had become primarily a big business rather than a spiritual community. I subscribed wholeheartedly to Eugene Peterson's observation, "The pastor's responsibility is to keep the community attentive to God."[2] This aspect of pastoral work was foundational to me. Sadly, this task did not often take priority and did not square with what churches really wanted. Keeping a congregation attentive to God's presence was often shuffled aside in order to tend to the "necessaries": budgets and finance, staff and personnel, maintenance of facilities, and the never-ending quest to keep all the plates spinning on a weekly basis. Admittedly, these responsibilities come with the territory, and they are a given in pastoral leadership. When these tasks take precedence, however, a church focuses its energy inward instead of outward. When these tasks move to the top of the list, they drive the agenda at the expense of making disciples, fostering deeper community, and discerning God's will for the congregation. "Keeping the community attentive to God" typically wound up at the bottom of the heap.

Here's an illustration. In my career, I have interviewed with a number of pastor search committees. The members have invariably asked me to recite my life story and my testimony of how I came to faith. They have asked about my family. I have answered questions about my strengths and weaknesses, leadership style, and staff relations. And of course, there were those ticklish questions about my stance on controversial issues. Without a doubt, these concerns were vitally important to the process, but they had a "transactional" feel to them: we ask, you answer, and we'll decide if we'll call you. To this day, I have never had a search committee ask me about my walk with God at a particular point in my life, nor have they inquired about the shape and texture of my faith. They have not asked about the things that have stretched my faith and my soul or the questions or doubts that have troubled me through the years. From this experience, I have concluded that many churches tend to place a premium on management rather than spirituality.

Equally frustrating is the resistance to change within churches. Congregations often say they want significant change but are either unwilling or unprepared to endure the discomfort that true change requires. Hidden commitments create an immunity to change. Time and again, I found the following axiom to be all too true: "Everyone is for change as long as everything remains the same!" Systems naturally seek homeostasis; they resist change and seek whatever is normal. In that light, despite the development of a list of core values and mission and vision statements, too often the real mission of the church is to keep things the way they are or seek a return to imagined glory days. One writer put it well: "Behavior sets standards, not ideals."[3] The way a church acts reveals its true understanding of its mission. Our actions, not our statements, reveal what we're after. Genuine alignment between proclamation and progress is hard to attain.

At this point, I must acknowledge that I have at times been a co-conspirator in this state of affairs. Typically, when I assumed a new pastorate, I moved slowly, wanting to get the lay of the land and get to know people rather than charging in with an agenda of my own. I did not want the congregation to assume that I had been to the mountaintop and had received a divinely ordained plan for the church's future. This stance has served me well. The downside of this strategy, however, is that by the time I had gained the trust of a congregation, I often had become enmeshed in the system. Being "together but separate," as Peter Steinke puts it, became an increasingly difficult balance to maintain, and I did not always manage the task well.[4] Once I became overly identified with a church's system, it was harder for me to change and thus provoke others to change.

I also wanted to be liked. Lewis Smedes, the longtime professor of theology and ethics at Fuller Seminary, offered up this gem: "Half of our struggle in growing up is coming to terms with the real reasons we have (and often hide) for doing the things we do."[5] I suspect that, beneath the surface, most ministers harbor a desire to be liked. Although we may not be able to put it into words (or don't want to!), the truth is that our call comes wrapped up with a desire for approval. While we genuinely wish to serve and bring a measure of hope and love to this world, we also wish to win the congregation's approval. We go about our work hoping at some level to receive positive strokes and obtain a blessing. I know I did. I was keenly self-aware that in trying to serve God's kingdom I was also hoping to get something out of it for myself, whether it be an accolade or a demonstration of love. Taken together, I wanted to fit in and belong instead of defining myself and encouraging the congregational system to adapt to me. I also wanted to be well thought of. My "real reasons" for doing my work were not always entirely pure and were hemmed in with self-interest (I'm not alone here—I'm convinced this is true for all of us). These tendencies frustrated my ability to work for significant change within a congregational system.

Compounding my restlessness was the fact that I was growing increasingly uncomfortable with the prevalent transactional and consumer-driven approach to faith. In that vein, Dallas Willard was right on target when he observed that the church had bought into the gospel of "sin management"—the notion that the Christian faith is all about being forgiven.[6] Forgiveness is important, but is that the sum total of the Christian faith? Is being a follower of Jesus Christ solely about being forgiven?

In this regard, I ran headlong into the widespread view that the most important thing was to "invite Jesus into your heart." Is that all it takes to become a Christian? "Inviting Jesus into your heart" by praying a simple prayer smacks of magic. One moment, you're out; the next moment, you're in! In my reading of the New Testament, I found no instances of people coming to faith by "asking Jesus into their hearts." The closest parallel appears in the letter to the church at Laodicea as recorded in Revelation 3:20: "Listen! I am standing at the door knocking; if you hear my voice and open the door, I will come in to you and eat with you and you with me." Despite the intimacy of this image, it is not a portrayal of coming to faith but instead is an encouragement for followers of Jesus to repent! Still, this language had taken hold and was hard to uproot. "Inviting Jesus into the heart," in my mind, reduced discipleship to an affair of the heart with little or no connection to daily living.

Likewise, I was increasingly uncomfortable with the church's pursuit of quick fixes.[7] Case in point: over the last several decades we have witnessed the rise of many megachurches in North America. A fixture of most of these churches is a "contemporary" style of worship in which a praise band takes the place of a choir, the preacher dons jeans and a camp shirt as opposed to a robe or a suit and tie, and multimedia technology drives the service. Please don't misunderstand my description. It is absolutely imperative for churches to understand the context in which they minister. It is also vital for the church to speak the language of its neighbors. Nevertheless, as many traditional churches grappled with a plateaued or declining membership, they assumed that the solution was to adopt this form of worship either by ditching traditional worship or adding a contemporary service. The working assumption was that having a contemporary service was the answer to all the church's problems! If we just do this, we'll grow! This preoccupation with method and technique is symptomatic of our technologically oriented and results-driven society. While taking stock of the best practices of others, we cannot simply assume that what works for another congregation will work for ours. There's no substitute for a congregation making the effort to know itself well and identify what makes it unique. Effective churches know who they are, and they claim their identity and gifts. They minister, serve, and worship, not by chasing after the latest trend but out of their uniqueness and with a keen awareness of their context.

This is but one example of the "quick fix" mentality rampant in our churches. Anxiety over the church's declining influence often manifests itself in the search for solutions rather than the searching of the soul. Leading a congregation to address the tension between these two approaches is a challenge all ministers face.

Something else was also buzzing in my head. I have always enjoyed the preaching task. Throughout my ministry, I have given it priority. I relished the research, writing, and refinement necessary for good preaching. Speaking to a congregation on Sundays was often the high point of my week. In fact, when I openly declared that I thought God was calling me, I remember telling my pastor that "I was being called to preach." That was it—nothing else! From the beginning, that was what I longed to do. This component of my call has not diminished in the slightest. I still relish preaching.

Nevertheless, I began to realize that I was hungry for more than simply speaking *to* a congregation. I longed for meaningful conversations *with* individuals. I wanted to engage with others on a more personal level about matters of faith. Let me be clear at this point. Throughout my work as a pastor, I have spoken with many people about some difficulty in their lives. I have been privileged to listen as others shared their grief, lamented the state of their marriages or their difficulties with their children, and navigated the harsh terrain of a crisis. I have also been privileged to be with those who gave up this life and stepped into the next. I rejoiced as I led two people to commit themselves to a lifetime together. These events were tremendously rewarding—they scratched my itch to be helpful and needed.

What was rare, however, was engaging another person in a serious and thoughtful conversation about their faith. Here's what I mean. I well remember the day I got a phone call from a church member. He wanted to meet for lunch, and he gave no hint about the reason for getting together. Since he was something of a pillar in the church, I immediately assumed there was some problem to be addressed or some issue to be resolved. Imagine my surprise when we sat down to lunch and he explained why he wanted to meet. He said, "Bill, I want to talk to you about my prayer life." This individual lived with chronic pain and had endured countless surgeries. Pain had driven him to be more and more prayerful. Despite his faithful practice, he wanted to talk about some steps he could take to enrich his prayer life. He wanted to be able to pray through his pain. We had a wonderful conversation and became soul friends. Sadly, such occurrences are all too rare.

Finally, and most significantly, I realized that I was undergoing a conversion of sorts. Some of my perspectives about ministry and congregational life were shifting. For example, I found myself at odds with the binary thinking that exists in much of religious life. Massive cultural shifts have injected an enormous sense of disquiet into churches. In the face of overwhelming change, the church has allowed itself to be overtaken by fear. We circle the wagons to keep the world from intruding. Congregations then embark on a quest for certainty. This search for certitude frequently manifests itself in either/or thinking. How many times have anxious members urged leaders to "draw a line in the sand" or "make a stand"? I frequently asked myself, "Do we have to frame everything in terms of 'this or that'?" Isn't there room for wondering as opposed to straight-line approaches? As I saw it, space for engaging the imagination was limited. Our horizons were too low. I was convinced that either/or thinking would lead only to a dead end. Unless we humbly admitted what we didn't know, we would stand little chance of bearing effective witness in a world where lots of people were searching for a sense of depth and purpose in life.

To summarize, something was stirring inside me. I was experiencing a "holy dissatisfaction" with the way things were. In Richard Rohr's terms, I was "falling upward."[8] His observation spoke volumes to me:

> In the first half of life, we fight the devil and have the illusion and inflation of "winning" now and then; in the second half of life, we always lose because we are fighting God. *The first battles solidify the ego and create a stalwart and loyal soldier; the second battles defeat the ego because God always wins.* No wonder so few want to let go of their loyal soldier; no wonder so few have the faith to grow up. The ego hates losing, even to God.[9]

For much of my life I had indeed been the "loyal soldier." At this stage of my life, however, I was indeed fighting and wrestling with God. I was on a growing edge, and it was extremely uncomfortable.

This soul struggle led to a significant decision. I had been privileged to serve as pastor of Ardmore Baptist Church in Winston-Salem, North Carolina. Together we had accomplished some wonderful things that bore positive witness to God's kingdom. After eleven years, however, I began to explore some of the questions I mentioned above. I felt restless and began trying to figure out what was going on within me. In response, I did what many pastors have done when facing this kind of discomfort. I interpreted my disquiet as a sign that I was ready for change and needed to move on. I began to let it be known to my network of colleagues and friends that I was open to making a move to another congregation. In hindsight, I think I really wanted and needed some time apart to think through some of these questions at a deeper level.

Nevertheless, in 2010, I received a call from First Baptist Church in Dalton, Georgia. The manner in which this opportunity came forth spoke to my family. We sensed the working of the Spirit. Ginny and I were excited about the possibilities, and our daughter, Mary Virginia, was willing to make the move even though she would be a senior in high school that year. We moved to Dalton, and everything went well for a while. I was heavily invested in bringing new staff on board—at least five searches in as many years! Ginny found a job leading a local nonprofit agency whose mission she resonated with strongly. As well, our move to Dalton was positive for Mary Virginia. She made lifelong friends in Dalton, and as a result of our living in Georgia, she decided to attend Mercer University, where she thrived and began to find her way into adulthood. All was indeed well—or so I thought.

Prior to my arrival, the church had taken on a heavy debt load. The anxiety over our indebtedness was exacerbated by the Great Recession. The anxiety was palpable, and it was the driver in virtually every aspect of the church's life, dictating what we could and could not do. In addition, there were a host of structural problems to be addressed with regard to staff alignment, operations, and finances. I jumped into these matters and did my best to fix as much as I could. I likened this work to car repair. There was a lot under the hood that needed to be fixed before things could run well. It's not the kind of work that's highly visible, nor does it create a lot of excitement. Still, it was necessary. Over time, I began to feel the effects of not working out of my strengths. My joy began to ebb away. I was doing what needed to be done, but it wasn't the kind of stuff that generated a great deal of excitement for me or the congregation. About four or five years in, I became aware of some congregational expectations I was not fulfilling. What needed to be done and what the church wanted done weren't always in sync. I entertained the thought that I wasn't a good fit for the church.

This state of affairs was exacerbated by a surprising turn of events. In 2014, Alan Culpepper announced his intention to retire from his position as the dean of the McAfee School of Theology. Given my status as a member of the Board of Trustees for the university, I was asked to serve on the search team for a new dean, a task I happily accepted. As the search unfolded, a colleague asked if he could recommend me for the position. I immediately said "yes" and then removed myself from the search team. The search team eventually came up with a list of five candidates for the position, and I was one of the five! I was thrilled beyond measure at the opportunity to interview, and I began making a rough outline of my aspirations for the school. The big day came, and I was interviewed by the search team. I thought the conversation went well, and Ginny and I allowed ourselves to daydream about what could be. Sadly, I was informed at the end of that day that I didn't make the cut to the final three. It was a major letdown! Although I didn't get the job, my excitement about the possibility shouted at me: "If I'm this excited about the possibility, what is that saying to me about where I am and what I ought to be doing?" This opportunity made me aware that I was yearning for something different.

I think the church picked up on that. Shortly thereafter, I began to receive strong criticism from some of the leadership in the church. Some of it was justified; much of it was not. Nevertheless, the experience was intense. With the help of an insightful leadership coach, I attempted to craft a way forward, but nothing worked. In fact, the more I talked with leadership, the worse things got. My world was crumbling, and I kept thinking, "This isn't supposed to happen to me!" I had a lot of restless and sleepless nights. Ginny, Mary Virginia, and I had more than a few long conversations about what was next. They, along with my dearest friends, were genuinely worried about me. They were fearful of the toll the stress was taking on me. A close friend, Jerry Mantooth, put it bluntly: "If you stay there, you will die." That got my attention! My conversations with my family, my friends, my coach, and my spiritual director all led me to the conclusion that I needed to step away.

Reflecting on this decision, I was drawn to Mark's account of the Lord's baptism and temptation. As Mark tells it—in his usual terse, no-frills, just-the-facts manner—Jesus submitted to baptism by John. Mark offers no explanation for Jesus' decision, and he offers no insight as to why Jesus felt compelled to wade into the water with John. All Mark tells us is that Jesus did, and John immersed Jesus in the waters.

When Jesus came up out of the water, he was dripping wet from head to toe. He took a moment to wipe the water from his eyes. John embraced him, and they looked at each other with knowing smiles. At that moment, as Mark tells it, the heavens were ripped open so that there was no distance between heaven and earth. In that one incredible instant, heaven and earth kissed. The great gulf between here and there disappeared. As a sign of this incredible breakthrough, the Holy Spirit lighted on Jesus as gently as a dove. All these signs signaled that this was indeed a one-of-a-kind moment, something that would never be repeated. The high point of this singular moment was that, right then and there, Jesus heard God speak to him. Jesus heard God speak a blessing upon him: "You are my beloved son; with you I am well pleased." We might render it this way: "You're mine, and I am so proud of you for doing the right thing!"

I bet when Jesus heard that, he grinned from ear to ear. I imagine he almost walked on water for the first time! God had given the blessing, and Jesus felt God's delight dripping all over him. He would never forget that day, and if we had been there, we would likely have thrown Jesus some kind of party. It was a moment to be savored.

But, as Mark tells it, there was no time for that.

The moment, as rich and powerful as it was, didn't last long. Mark writes that no sooner had Jesus come out of the water and heard God's blessing than the Holy Spirit "immediately" (that's one of Mark's favorite words) cast Jesus into the wilderness. Instead of launching directly into his ministry, Jesus was driven out into the desert.

Linger over that word "driven" (*ekbállei*) or "cast out" for a moment. It's the same word Mark frequently uses to describe exorcisms—those occasions when Jesus drove evil spirits out of people. It's not a gentle word. In fact, it carries more than a hint of violence. Thus, Mark paints a picture of the Holy Spirit picking Jesus up by the back of the neck and hurling him into the vast emptiness of the desert. In other words, Jesus didn't *choose* to go there; the Spirit *drove* him there. The Holy Spirit took Jesus someplace he didn't necessarily want to go.

That's an accurate description of my experience. Although the decision to leave was mine, I sensed the Holy Spirit driving me. At the end of January 2016, I resigned as pastor and walked away. The decision took me not where I wanted to go but certainly where I needed to go. In taking that fateful step, little did I know I was stepping into the wilderness.

QUESTIONS FOR REFLECTION

1. Can you make a distinction between saying "I quit" and saying "I've had enough"?

2. What frustrates you where you are? How do you cope? How does this speak to your life?

3. Describe an instance when you sensed the Spirit was leading you someplace you didn't want to go?

CHAPTER 2

WANDERING

For the Israelites traveled forty years in the wilderness....
—Joshua 5:6a

If you don't know the end of the story, you're still trapped in it.
—*Herrens Veje*, season 1, episode 3

Initially, stepping aside gave me a great deal of relief. I literally felt the weight fall off my shoulders. After all, for more than forty years, I had been on call. As with all pastors, I had visited hospitals and other healthcare facilities innumerable times. The phone often rang in the middle of the night, prompting me to get out of bed, get my clothes on, and head somewhere. I had witnessed more tragedies than I could count. I had the privilege of witnessing others pass from this life to the next and faced the challenge of rising to the occasion both in offering pastoral care and in conducting a funeral. And who knows how many hours I had invested in staff meetings, committee meetings, team meetings, and any other kind of meeting one could imagine! Vacations were interrupted, and it was nigh impossible to plan a vacation or time off without a lot of preparation. Spontaneity was not the name of the game! As well, for forty years I had worked the Sunday-to-Sunday grind of preparing sermons and Bible studies. There's a lot of truth in the adage, "Sunday's always coming." Walking away allowed me to catch my breath.

My decision also offered a bonus. For the first time in a long while, I was able to spend uninterrupted time with my family. Aside from a three-month sabbatical in 2006, time together was hard to come by. At this point, Mary Virginia had graduated from Mercer and had moved to Tuscaloosa to purse a master's degree at the University of Alabama. Ginny and I were free to visit her any time we wished, and we did! We went to ball games, gymnastics competitions, and theater productions. Priceless! Ginny and I were also able to travel a bit. We knew we needed to get away and lose ourselves in some new scenery. Putting physical space between us and our last pastorate allowed us to breathe.

As with the children of Israel, we were glad to be out of Egypt's land. But an unanswered question always lingered just beneath the surface: what's next? Where do we go, and how do we get there? We were on the fringe of the wilderness. Or, as William Bridges puts it, we were in the "neutral zone."[10] We had had our ending and had indeed let go of something important, but we had no idea what the future held. We were definitely in between "the old reality and the new one."[11]

This awareness figured prominently in several important decisions as we attempted to embrace our new life. First, we knew we needed to move, but where? We recognized we needed to put physical distance between the church and ourselves. The longer we stayed, the more awkward chance meetings with church members became. Once we got past the usual "how are you?" and "what are you doing?" questions, the conversations trailed off in uneasy silence. If we were truly going to walk away, we needed to move. This was important for both us and the church. My decision to leave came as a shock to many, and the church needed to do a postmortem and have some thoughtful conversations about their future. That process would best be served by my absence. Certainly, they didn't need me to have a front-row seat as they began to search for a new pastor!

All this to say, we knew we needed to move, but where? Since I didn't have a job, deciding where to land was a serious decision. And we didn't know whether to buy a home or rent one. In our minds, the prospect of buying a new home, settling in, and then perhaps landing a job that would require yet another move was unappealing to say the least. We opted to move to Chattanooga since that was our least disruptive option. For the time being, we also determined that we would rent—we wanted to be ready for the next move whenever and wherever a job came open for me.

As important as the physical relocation was, I soon learned that I was also facing a spiritual relocation. My first soul crisis was one of identity: I realized I did not know how *not* to be a minister. Ministry was not only what I did but also who I was. In the Danish television series *Herrens Veje*, the central character is a minister in the state church of Denmark. His name is Johannes Krogh. In the final episode, he is forced to resign his position as dean of the churches in his parish. A conversation between Krogh and his wife resonated with me: "If I'm not this, then I don't know what I am."[12] If I'm not a pastor, I don't know who I am. That was the first symptom of my "lostness."

That sense of "lostness" also made an appearance on Easter Sunday 2016. Since we were relocating to Chattanooga, we had not yet found a faith community. Holy Week began, and we realized we had no place to go on Easter Sunday. We gave the matter a lot of thought and decided we would worship at the First United Methodist Church in Dalton. Their pastor, Robin Lindsey, had been a stalwart friend and confidant. He genuinely loved us, and we loved him in return. So we went.

As the service got underway, I was overwhelmed by a wave of pent-up emotion. I broke down and wept. For the first time in forever, I was not in the pulpit on Easter proclaiming the good news of Jesus' resurrection. That hurt! Ginny and Mary Virginia held my hands tightly and shed their own tears. From his perch on the platform, Robin took notice of this family drama, and during the recessional he paused for a moment and put his hand on my shoulder. He gave us all a gentle gaze, a look full of empathy and understanding. He gave us a gift we all needed right then and there. At that moment, I realized I didn't know how to go forward or create a new identity.

When we finally moved to Chattanooga, we visited several churches searching for a place to belong. Invariably, when the minister preached, it was all I could do not to leave my pew and storm the pulpit and "fix" the sermon! On several occasions, Ginny sensed my rising tension and discomfort, and she gently squeezed my knee to calm me down. I was a lousy pew-sitter! Such occurrences reminded me that I was a preacher at heart! That was my calling. That was my gift. Not being able to preach made me miserable. I couldn't be who I was or use the gifts I knew I had.

These experiences propelled and intensified my search for what was next. Initially, I thought I was on my way to a teaching post. The day after I left the church, Rob Nash, then the interim dean of the McAfee School of Theology, called and offered me a position as an adjunct New Testament professor for the fall. I accepted his offer immediately, and I quickly came to the conclusion that this was bound to be my new calling. Surely, everything up to now was leading to this. I firmly believed this was where my experience was taking me. After all, I had a good track record of teaching at both the undergraduate and graduate level, and I loved it! I consistently received solid reviews from students about my classroom presence. This development lined up with and confirmed something I had heard from many friends for a long time: "You'll teach!" In every church I served, many members offered glowing affirmation about my ability to teach. In fact, many of the folks in Dalton believed that this was indeed my true calling. It looked like an obvious open door.

Thus, I devoted summer 2016 to preparing lectures for an upper-level elective on the Gospel of Mark. I had to do some catching up and spent a lot of time reading. In addition, I began to design my approach to the class with a view toward linking the content to the students' vocational call. I did not want simply to be a conveyor of information; I wanted my students to engage the Gospel in terms of the ministry they aspired to. I had some wonderful students, and, frankly, I had a ball leading the class. Encouraged by this rich experience, I met with the new dean in late fall and inquired about a full-time teaching post. He informed me that there was no opening. My heart sank. To say I was disappointed doesn't even begin to describe my feeling. What I assumed to be an open door quickly closed. I had to focus my attention elsewhere.

All the while, I continued to submit my name for open pulpits and other jobs in Baptist life. I got a few looks from some churches but never emerged as a top candidate. This turn of events was likely providential; in hindsight, I don't think I was ready for a new pastorate. I felt very fragile. Sadly, I concluded that many thought I was too old—past my "sell by" date. I also realized that many were likely to view me as damaged goods. Even though I had a wealth of experience and a ton of energy to burn, I had no takers. I felt like a castoff.

My next step was to seek a job outside of ministry. I figured a lot of the skills I possessed as a minister would easily translate to secular work. I hadn't applied for a job since I was in my twenties, and thus I had no clue how to navigate the job market. Consequently, I secured the services of a career coach. She helped me update my resume to fit possible jobs and created a personal profile that called attention to my capabilities. That done, she began to search for openings that matched my skill set. I thought I was on my way somewhere. Once again, however, disappointment showed up. During one of our sessions, my coach greeted me with the news that her searches had come up empty. She also acknowledged that she didn't know what to do for an out-of-work minister. We parted company, and I began to search for a job on my own.

I have to say this was an extraordinarily frustrating process. I quickly learned that the old days of reading about a job opening and setting up an appointment for an interview were gone. The whole application process was now an online venture. As a result, I became well acquainted with websites such as Work for Good, ZipRecruiter, Indeed, and LinkedIn and some university-based job boards. To get started, I set filters to narrow down the jobs I might like. When promising jobs popped up, I applied. I quickly learned that these job sites employ their own unique algorithms. If an application or resume doesn't hit on certain words, the application disappears into internet ether. Equally maddening was the experience of being considered yet not finding out about the status of my application for months. Please, somebody, get me a human! From 2017 to 2018, I applied for more than fifty jobs—everything from part-time to full-time.[13] The low point came when I didn't even rate a call back from a pharmacy to deliver prescriptions! For many jobs, I was overqualified in terms of my education and experience. I didn't make the cut for some jobs because I was underqualified. I didn't have the appropriate technical training or lacked certification in some area that was essential to the job. I was getting nowhere fast!

A maddening pattern emerged. When a live opportunity opened up, I decided to put my search on hold until I got a firm answer. Time and again, when I thought doors were about to swing open, they slammed shut. I got my hopes up only for them to be dashed. My life mirrored the instructions on a shampoo bottle: wash, rinse, and repeat.

Before making the decision to step away as a pastor, I had been rereading the letters to the seven churches in Revelation. The letter to the church at Philadelphia riveted my attention: "I know your works. Look, I have set before you an open door, which no one is able to shut."[14] At the time, I took this verse as something of a promise. Stepping aside would lead to other open doors. I assumed that somewhere not too far off was a door that had been propped open for me. Thus far, however, I had encountered one closed door after another. I was living the age-old question: how much is God's part and how much is mine? How do I strike a balance between waiting on the Lord and taking charge myself?

This state of affairs made me wonder if God knew I was alive. I questioned whether my prayers made any difference. I grew weary of well-meaning people telling me, "The Lord has something special in mind for you." If God did indeed have something special out there, why couldn't I get to it? Why did this thing tarry? Why was I consigned to such eternal waiting? These and other questions surfaced frequently, and my prayers reflected this (more about that in the next chapter).

To make matters worse, I suffered a triple compound fracture of my right ankle in January 2018. The surgery to repair my ankle went well, but I was essentially confined to bed (or the couch). I couldn't put any weight on my right ankle for four solid months. Once again, my life was on hold. I couldn't plan much of anything, and my days were marked by an aggravating sense of sameness. To be confined in this manner was a living hell for me. By temperament, I am geared for action. I am always asking, "What's next?" I derive immense satisfaction from getting things done.

As frustrating as this predicament was, it was not without value. Being hobbled taught me invaluable lessons. For example, healing takes its own time. The process can't be rushed or sped up. Giving things time is the name of the game. I also learned what it's like to be dependent on others. I had to be waited on and tended to. I experienced firsthand what life was like for those whom I had visited in similar circumstances. And, most important, being hobbled in this manner was a metaphor for my life. Not only was my ankle broken; *I* was broken. Not only was my ankle dislocated in the worst possible way; *I* was dislocated. I couldn't take charge and make something happen—I had to sit and wait for things to take their course.

The result of this aimless wandering was that I rented out too much space for unhealthy self-recrimination. I began to hear myself saying, "You're a failure!" "You have really messed up, and there's no way out!" "You're not as gifted as you think you are!" Try as I might, I couldn't escape this self-labeling. To tell the truth, I realized that I had never really been in a tough spot before—the kind that tests everything in you. Let me call your attention to the epigraph that headlines this chapter: "If you don't know the end of the story, you're still trapped in it."[15] My story thus far had no end, and I was indeed trapped in it. Previously, I could have plotted my life in a fairly straight line with an upward trajectory. Now the path of life looked like a bunch of squiggles with no discernible pattern. Thus far, I had encountered roadblocks, had ventured into dead ends, and had collided head on with unyielding and unpleasant realities. The end of my story was nowhere in sight, and my soul was withering.

I was in the thickest part of the wilderness and couldn't find my way out.

QUESTIONS FOR REFLECTION

1. Have you ever been in the wilderness? Describe that experience. What was it like?

2. What alerted you to the fact that you were indeed wandering without a map?

3. What kinds of prayers did you offer? How much did you leave in God's hands, and how much did you take into your own? How did this tension play out for you?

CHAPTER 3

THIRSTING

As the deer longs for flowing streams, so my soul longs for you, O God.
—Psalm 42:1

When you cannot pray as you would, pray as you can.
—Harry Emerson Fosdick,
The Meaning of Prayer[16]

The wilderness is first and foremost a place of prayer. Wandering through the wilderness strips off the veneer of our comfortable spirituality and lays bare what truly resides in the soul. The wilderness, however, also confronts us with a paradox. Although our time in hard and barren places makes us thirsty for God and God alone, God remains elusive. Silence is the frequent answer to our most passionate prayers and longings.

In this chapter, I illustrate my thirst for God in three ways. First, I open my journal to you and let you see my record of some events from 2015 to early 2020. I have been selective here and have chosen entries that illustrate how I wound up in the wilderness and what I experienced there.

Second, I offer some prayers from my journal. On numerous occasions my words caught in my throat when I tried to speak to God. Writing thus became the medium through which I offered my prayers. I include some of my prayers and reflections here based on my Scripture reading for a particular day.

Third, like so many who have worked hard to make sense of their lives, I have found much consolation in the book of Job. I have read portions of Job on and off since 2015. Early in 2019, I took a deep dive into the book in hopes that Job's collision with age-old questions might benefit me. And it did! Thus, I offer reflections on selected texts that I have found particularly helpful.

I conclude this chapter with some of the "big ideas" that surfaced along the way.

EVENTS

May 7, 2015

Meetings with my spiritual director, Julie Johnson, have been life-giving. Our conversation yesterday was no exception. Here's a summary:

- She thought that the signs had aligned just right for me to become dean at McAfee. Since things did not work out as we both hoped, she reminded me that God has to work with a lot of moving parts, and thus what we believe is right may not come to fruition.
- The joy I felt in getting an interview for the deanship was a sure sign that I was being released from my call. That may indeed be true. Of late I have felt that I haven't been able to use my best gifts.
- She observed that May is my "crappy" month. It was crappy last year and probably the year before that. She suggested I give some thought to figure out how to do some "sliding and gliding" in May rather than cranking up the intensity.

Our vacation is a few weeks away, I am looking forward to getting away. I think we all are.

May 17, 2015

I have edited this entry in order to maintain confidentiality.

Yesterday the roof fell in on me. I met with three members of our Staff Committee. During the meeting, they raised three issues with me. Any one of those items was more than enough for a single conversation, yet they unloaded all three at once!

The first concern was bogus. If they truly believed it, they would have focused the conversation on that issue alone. The other two were offered in vague generalities. Without concrete examples, I can't do anything—I don't know exactly what they want me to work on.

This conversation may be a sign I'm done here. At the very least, I am now forced to reevaluate my calling and my place here. As well, are these issues representative of the church-at-large or just a few?

Still, I feel like I have been kicked in the gut. Everything is suddenly up for grabs. Do I need to resign? Is this eruption really all about me, or does it point to something else? I feel very, very fragile. I'm certainly in a place where I need God's wisdom and help.

June 24, 2015

As hard as it is for me to envision, I may be on my way out of here. That realization prompts a lot of questions. Why hasn't this worked? Why have I not been able to connect with this church as I have with others?

Right now, I have zero motivation. Yet, I can't give up. I have to find a way to keep moving and doing my best. Still, it's very hard. I never imagined I would find myself in this spot.

July 17, 2015

Despite the ongoing conversations with the Staff Committee, I feel OK at this point. A mix of freedom, relief, and some anxiety about the future. I have to hold on to the fact that this really isn't about me in its entirety. I have to hold on to the fact that God can use this mess for good.

August 30, 2015

Serving as a pastor has been hard and difficult at times, but on the whole quite rewarding. I have a treasure trove of memories of good people I've met. Plus, I am well aware of the good things that have been accomplished in the congregations I've served and ways I have positively influenced others. Moreover, I have a wealth of friends.

But now it appears the time has come for me to explore new avenues. For maybe the first time in a long time, I'm moving from my obligation "to do what I'm supposed to do" to letting my life tell me what it wants to do. Maybe this is a lesson I should have learned a long time ago, but that does not mean my life up to now has been without value and significance. Perhaps I have finally let God's "goodness and mercy" catch up with me. This turn of events may be signaling that my calling is perhaps being redirected and seeking a fresh expression.

September 7, 2015

At the close of yesterday's service, I heard the following comments: "You have brought so much light to this place." "That was one from the heart!" "I don't know why someone isn't overwhelmed with God's Spirit!"

I realize that's a small sample, but it does make me wonder if the Staff Committee has heard this. At least a few people think I'm doing a good job! In light of this, Ginny was wondering last night if it was possible the Staff Committee might have a change of heart if they had heard comments such as these. I am of the opinion it would take a great deal of spiritual discernment and no small dose of humility on their part to do that. May the Lord's will be done!

September 10, 2015
Yesterday was a rough day.

When I met with the Staff Committee, they pushed me hard to make a decision about my future. They pressed me hard to assess the status of my calling. The entire experience was very intense and very uncomfortable; at times I felt I was being interrogated. They don't get that this is an intensely spiritual search for me. Nor do they understand that I'm trying to discern whether I'm really done or if there is a hopeful way forward. I know I've given mixed signals, but that is merely the outward expression of the stuff churning inside me. Apparently, they want a clear-cut answer right now! How can I offer that when I've been in a state of upheaval since May?

I'm shaky and worn out emotionally. I don't know how I'm going to muster the strength to preach Sunday.

November 13, 2015

I have finally come to the conclusion that the best choice for me (and for the church) is for me to resign. That will likely not take place until the end of January. As scary as it is, I think it's the right thing to do. Yesterday, when I spoke with my best friend from seminary days, Jerry Mantooth, he gave me his full support—insisting that if I don't leave, I'll die. That certainly puts things into perspective!

The biggest challenge? Framing my resignation to the church in terms that honor as much truth as I can tell and lessen the harm. Although I have ample reason to be angry (and I am!), throwing people under the bus will not serve me or the church.

If I think about this too much, I can get scared [expletive deleted]. Still, I believe staying will only cause me to be even more frustrated. Beyond January, I can't think too far ahead. Ginny and I are really walking off the map, and we have no idea where we're headed or what awaits us. I suppose this is the biggest step of faith I've ever taken.

January 1, 2016

Today is my 60th birthday. Oddly enough, I don't feel that old, although a glance in the mirror tells me that Father Time has not ignored me! I have 60 years of accumulated experience and memories. By far the majority of them are extremely positive. Mom and Dad gave me a good foundation, lots of opportunities to try things, and loads of love. I have followed my calling as I have had light to see, and for the most part, I believe I have been faithful. I am a good minister, and I believe strongly that I have nudged others into God's kingdom. My prayer is that I have made this world a better place.

All that said, I am on the precipice of a new adventure. I am charting a new course, willing to risk doing something new. I don't know where it will take me or what I will do. I do know that this is a huge step of faith. It is exciting and scary all at the same time.

February 2, 2016

Sunday the 31st was my last day. I left with a mixture of emotions: sadness, anger, and relief. Although I am sure I will miss pastoral work, I am glad to be out of this situation. I probably won't understand for a long time what really led to this moment. I trust in time I will see and be at peace.

This turn of events has uncovered how much "success" means to me. Although I know at some level I didn't fail, I truly thought this would never happen to me. Even more perplexing is the fact that I think I'm at my best right now in many ways, particularly preaching.

God's good timing! Yesterday, the 1st, I received a call from Rob Nash at McAfee, asking if I would be willing to teach in the fall. This is great news! His invitation and the timing of it was real shot in the arm. Boosted my spirit enormously.

February 22, 2016

My reading today was from Mark 9:14-29—the story of Jesus cleansing a young boy who was possessed by an unclean spirit. Some thoughts and observations:

Jesus' healing of this child was violent. The evil spirit put up quite a fight and mightily resisted being cast out. In fact, the spirit's departure left the boy in what appeared to be a lifeless state. It was a healing nigh unto death.

This captures the state of affairs in my own soul right now. I am being healed. But the healing has been violent and not without cost. I feel that much that defined me has been ripped out and thrown away. I am left wondering if I will ever rise again. Has the healing left me without a future as a minister? Or is this healing a prelude to something I can't yet imagine?

The story calls attention to the disciples' impotence; against the tenacity of this spirit, they could no nothing. Only Jesus was able to bring about his healing and restoration. It may have to be the same with me.

March 10, 2016

I keep trying to get ahead of myself by figuring out how things are supposed to play out over the next few months. Where am I going to wind up? What is my future? Where is life going to take me?

At the same time, however, my spirit frequently whispers to me that I may not be at all ready for anything new, not just yet. Still, I have such a desire to be settled. This is what Abraham and Sarah must have felt to some degree as they traveled, not knowing where they were headed or what their final destination would be. May it be so with me.

July 26, 2016

Preaching at Garden Lakes (where my good friend, Jimmy Gentry, serves as pastor) was fun and invigorating. I think I did well. Ginny says I belong in the pulpit. It sure felt good. Maybe this is one more piece in the puzzle of what's next. What am I to make of this? What does this event have to say about my future?

August 20, 2016

I have spent much of the time since my last entry reading and preparing for the class I will teach. Diving back into the deep waters of biblical scholarship has reminded me of how much there is to know and how little I actually know! Still, I have made good headway and have three lectures ready to go.

September 3, 2016

These last days have been filled with study, travel, and teaching. Some observations:

- Traveling back and forth from Chattanooga to Atlanta each Tuesday has shown me that I am not a road warrior! If I did this all the time, I think I would tire of it quickly.
- Ginny's sense of call is reawakening. She preached at the Lutheran church in Dalton and did an outstanding job. Can you imagine Lutherans clapping!? She has another opportunity in October. Something is up with her.
- I have enjoyed teaching my class and feel I'm growing into the role.
- I have had some additional opportunities to preach. I have enjoyed them immensely. It makes me wonder if I might be a pastor again.

December 4, 2016

Today's worship service was just what I needed. Thomas preached from Isaiah 11: "out of the stump a shoot will bloom." He linked the passage to the recent wildfires that raged in and around Gatlinburg. Out of what seems blackened and dead, new life will emerge. God brings new life and second chances. That is exactly where I'm living and what I am hoping for: the emergence of new life. That was gospel for me today!

January 2, 2017

I had a wonderful birthday yesterday. Lots of good wishes from friends.

Rick Bennett, the coordinator for the Tennessee CBF, spoke to me about an opening at one of the seminaries. He thought I'd be a good fit and asked if he could put my name in for a seminary job. I immediately said, "Yes!" If it turns out, this work would give me a chance to pass on some of my experience, perhaps teach some, and continue preaching. Obviously, this situation will take a while to develop but I do find it interesting and intriguing.

March 14, 2017

From a message I sent to my spiritual director, Julie Johnson: Here's the big "aha!" I don't think I want to be a full-time pastor anymore. Filling in, doing interims—that's all good. But to be back in the thick of it is not where I need to be. I have too many questions and no longer want to serve churches whose sole mission is "to get things back the way they used to be." I'm really OK with this.

June 30, 2017

I keep having dreams that are repetitive in nature. The dreams feature things that have to be negotiated over and over, sort of like Sisyphus pushing the rock up the hill repeatedly. I guess that's reflective of my sense of a lack of progress. I can't seem to get anywhere.

September 16, 2017

No one seems to be able to figure out why I haven't landed somewhere yet. I don't know whether to keep waiting or just do something, anything! Of late, I have had inquiries that buoyed my hopes and lifted my spirit. As a result, I put things on hold to see what will transpire. Those leads then disappear into a black hole and suddenly vanish—maddening! I find nothing but silence. I keep wondering if there is supposed to be some big "aha!" moment that brings it all together. So I keep plodding but my faith is wearing a bit thin. There are days when I think that this is just the way it's going to be.

December 19, 2017

I read through my journal the other day. This year has been hard. Lots of travel, two moves, a lot of energy spent getting settled, and a lot of closed doors. The coming year will have to be better.

February 10, 2018

It's been a little over two weeks since I had my accident: fell off a stepladder and broke my ankle in three places. I am happy to record that I am on the mend. I saw my doctor on the 8th, and he confirmed that I am indeed healing, but his biggest concern is the potential for infection.

I am learning that healing is a slow process. I won't be able to put any weight on my ankle until mid-April. The body heals at its own pace—nothing can make it speed up.

I have a wealth of friends. Via phone and social media I have heard from hundreds of people wishing me well. Many are actively praying for me. At such moments, one can never have too many people cheering you on from the sideline.

The best of all, however, is that I have an incredible wife and daughter! They have been as solid as a rock, and I love them all the more! I could not have asked for a more wonderful family.

This accident further complicates my efforts to get on with life. Still, I had some great news while waiting to see the doctor on the 8th. I opened an email indicating I had been accepted into Georgetown's Executive Leadership coaching program! I'd dance if I could! God moment? That gives me something to look forward to!

April 25, 2018

I attended my first session at Georgetown last week. Wow! What an incredible experience. There was such an impressive assortment of people from all different backgrounds. We bonded quickly. I do think I'm on the right track. The session was tremendously stimulating, and I ate it up. I'm a student at heart!

June 19, 2018

We had a fabulous time returning to Ardmore, my former pastorate. I was honored to lead worship, and the response was overwhelmingly positive. Ginny and I were in bad need of the load of affirmation and love we received. The appreciation was so heartfelt. The experience will stay with me for a long, long time.

June 26, 2018

In the story of the healing of Jairus's daughter in Mark 5, Mark observes that Jesus overheard the conclusion of the bystanders that the man's daughter was dead. Hearing that conclusion, Jesus overruled their assessment and insisted that another possibility should be considered. He said, "She is not dead, but sleeping." Jesus *overheard* their conclusion and stepped in to offer a fresh alternative.

Assuming the Lord overhears both what I say in my prayers and to others, what would he correct? What new possibility would he point out? How would he correct my understanding of where I am now?

July 7, 2018

A reflection on 2 Corinthians 12:2-10:

Although Paul speaks of his revelation, he doesn't elevate it unduly. Instead, he speaks of his weaknesses and infirmities. He sees his struggle and his weaknesses—in essence, his very humanity—as a truer prism through which to view God's sustaining grace. According to Paul, struggle and weakness bear more potential for experiencing God's grace than our highest moments.

This perspective runs so contrary to our culture of self-promotion. In today's world we have to put ourselves out there—usually in the best light possible. That's a strong tendency. Paul, however, insists that our failings, failures, and weaknesses allow God's grace to be experienced at a deeper level.

I have experienced the truth of Paul's affirmation. Certainly, I have been sustained by God's grace in ways known and unknown. I trust that my foray into the thicket of the wilderness has shaped me so that my life might offer a truer reflection of that same grace.

August 15, 2018

I got a nice lift yesterday. The book I finished in December 2014 has finally been published. I got the word yesterday and also received a stack of complimentary copies. Feels really good to hold the completed work in my hands and see it in print. I was so giddy yesterday I didn't get much done. Happily distracted!

October 8, 2018

A brief note on Psalm 66: "The Lord has brought me to a spacious place." A place where there's room to breathe. A place where all the constraints are removed. A place where one can move. This is what I long for.

October 31, 2018

After an eternity of waiting we learned that Ginny got the job as a hospice chaplain in Knoxville! That news came at just the right moment; it was a real shot in the arm. We have a lot to do to make the move, but that's a minor consideration in light of this joyous development.

November 27, 2018

Last night I got a call from the chair of an interim search team. I have an interview tentatively scheduled for next Wednesday evening. This may be a long hoped-for breakthrough. I am so grateful! If this opportunity does come to fruition, perhaps it will mark the end of my wilderness journey. [I interviewed and didn't receive further consideration.]

February 18, 2019

I need to write to settle my soul. Last week was encouraging. I learned that my name is before two or three churches in search of a pastor. The interims have put in a good word for me. There is another opportunity to work with pastors, and I intend to apply.

It's so encouraging to have some fresh possibilities. That said, these developments have stirred the fires of impatience. I'm ready to hear something. I am anxious to get on with things.

March 6, 2019

I reread my entry from this time last year. Healing was taking place, and I had made significant progress. And a year ago we closed on the purchase of our home. Who would have guessed that we'd be selling it and moving a year later? Crazy!

May 11, 2019

The weeks since my last entry have been filled with preparations for moving and executing the move itself. We are, at last, in our new home, and almost finished with the first phase of moving in.

The sheer exertion of packing and moving has left me exhausted. It's been a soul-killing grind.

May 29, 2019

Attended Ginny's first funeral service—she did an absolutely superb job. It's clear she's meant for this kind of work.

We drove to Chattanooga two weeks ago for her ordination council. It was a rich experience all around and very affirming for Ginny.

May 30, 2019

Some quotes from Anton Myrer's book, *Once an Eagle*, a novel that has been used at military academies to teach leadership:

- "The essence of leadership was an unerring ability to winnow the essential from the trivial or extraneous."
- "That's the whole challenge of life—to act with honor and hope and generosity, no matter what you've drawn. You can't help when or what you were born, you may not be able to help how you die; but you can—and should—try to pass the days between as a good man . . . ."
- "Maybe that was simply the price you paid for the truth; you exposed your own frailties along with others . . . ."

These quotes distill much that I've thought about over the last few years.

A big part of leadership for any minister is the ability to separate the essential from the extraneous. This has been at the heart of much of my uneasiness with congregational life these days. We major on minors and get tied up by things that don't matter much in the long run.

As well, I think I have attempted to pass my days here with "honor, hope, and generosity." These values were poured into my life's foundation from the beginning. My parents stressed the importance of keeping faith with myself and my best values. Hope has been a hallmark of my temperament; I deeply believe in God's power to create a future, especially when it doesn't seem possible. Although my hope has waxed and waned over the last few years, I have always come home to it. Generosity means that we are measured by what we give instead of what we receive. I have shared of my resources freely and have tried to give my life away on purpose.

Sadly, my efforts to live out these values have often been misinterpreted. My devotion to living honorably means that I seek to tell the truth. I have learned that for all our lip service to the truth, we don't always want to hear it. My kindness and generosity have been mistaken for weakness. When I have given praise to others and not put myself forward, I have been labeled a poor leader.

May 31, 2019

I vented my spleen to God today, employing some of Jeremiah's choice language! I am so weary of waiting. For the last 3+ years I have struggled with one key issue: figuring out when I'm supposed to wait on God and when I'm supposed to take the initiative. I still haven't figured that out, not by a long shot. Still, today I called on God to keep his promise to me—that there would be for me an open door that no one could shut.

June 7, 2019

My prayers of late have resulted in futility. Learned today that I didn't make the cut for another job. When it comes to God's part in this, it sure feels like God has gone off duty. Throughout my life, I have marked several "just in time" moments when the Lord came through for me. Now, however,

I only feel God's absence and seeming impotence. My prayers for work have been greeted with nothing but silence. I'm not sure I have much to say to God for the time being. This current state of affairs has gone on way too long. I think I've done my part to remain faithful, but at present I feel that my soul is very, very thin. I simply do not understand.

June 23, 2019

Lately I have had a couple of dreams featuring snakes! Really on the edge of *The Twilight Zone* here! Snakes, I learned, can be symbols of both our fears *and* our potential transformation. That explains why those dreams have showed up in my sleep. Over the last week, my anxiety has ramped up again. I have been and am still in the process of dying to what was in hopes that I might become something else.

June 28, 2019

Since late spring, I have been rereading Job. So much wisdom in such an ancient book! The book articulates many of my thoughts and emotions.

For example, I resonated with Job's words in 10:8-10. "You made me like a handcrafted piece of pottery—and now are you going to smash me to pieces?" That eloquent and honest statement has filtered through my mind many, many times. I have all these skills, gifts, and a breadth of wisdom and experience—are you going to let it all go to waste? Are you intent on smashing me to pieces?

July 9, 2019

Mary Virginia got her dream job at New York University! Proud!! She'll begin in August. Although we will lament the increased distance between us, we are thrilled she has this opportunity. This will make 5 moves for our family in the last 3+ years!

August 24, 2019

Got word I didn't get a job I had applied for. Once again, I'm living the "lather, rinse, repeat" routine. Here's the pattern: something hopeful pops up, I wait to see what will develop, and then the opportunity vanishes. Ginny has said repeatedly, "This makes no sense!" Didn't see this turn of events coming, not at all.

September 12, 2019

The last few weeks have been joyous in many ways.

- The reunion of my former youth group in Aberdeen, Mississippi, was a blast! So good to see how well so many of those youth are doing as adults! Very, very rewarding. Lots of laughter all around as we told stories and dug up old memories.
- Ginny's ordination last Sunday was simply beautiful. We had friends from all over on hand, and the service itself was incredibly moving. We are honored, humbled, and grateful.
- I begin this coming Sunday as the interim pastor at First Baptist in Erwin, Tennessee. This gets me back in the game! Very excited!

October 1, 2019

The interim work at First Baptist Church, Erwin has been delightful thus far, and the work has given me a great deal of joy and satisfaction. I am gaining their trust and acceptance. In particular, I have received much affirmation from several members about the way I handled a health emergency that occurred during the service. Thankfully, all turned out well.

October 24, 2019

I decided today to embark on an exercise of trust. I determined that I would cease praying about work and what's next. I've spoken to God about this ad infinitum. Surely, the Lord knows what I need. Although Jesus insisted on the importance of "asking, seeking, and knocking" and also the importance of "praying and not losing heart," I am weary of voicing the same prayers over and over. It is time to let all of this go and give it to God completely. This action is my declaration of my trust in God's timing and wisdom. We'll see how it goes.

November 23, 2019

The futility of my job search has forced me to think a lot about God. I realize that so much of my perception of God derives from my formative years. While I feel loved and valued, I also feel I have to be perfect—I have been weighed down with a lot of "shoulds." There are times I think God can't be gracious because I have made too many bad decisions or have exercised poor judgment. I imagine God saying, "I've given you all these chances. It's all your fault. There's nothing I can do to help." In my head I know that's not correct; still, I often *feel* that way.

Along those same lines, I have thought a lot about God's power. Scripture contains so many accounts of God's power at work; yet that immense power can't help me get a simple job. How do I square that? Of course, God is not Santa Claus. But some persistent questions keep tugging at my sleeve. Does following God and serving God mean that none of us can expect any return or blessing? What does that mean in terms of our prayers for others? Do our prayers have any effect at all? To frame the matter differently, "What am I supposed to do and what can I expect God to do?" I don't have any answers to those questions.

December 16, 2019

Yesterday was a very good day. The warmth and affection of the people at Erwin have blessed my soul. I revised my Advent sermon a bit to address their intention to call a new pastor. At the close of the worship service, the church voted to extend the call; that means I'll be out of work in a couple of weeks! It will be bittersweet to say goodbye to them. I will not miss the long drive, but I will miss them!

January 7, 2020

From my reading of Joshua 3, I have a mental picture of God standing in the midst of the Jordan River and holding back the waters so the Israelites could cross over. Because things remain tough, I long for God to hold the waters back so I can cross over to dry land and a new future. I remain doggedly hopeful that this will be the year my journey comes to a good end.

February 10, 2020

Last night I dreamed I was attempting to take off from a short airstrip surrounded by tall trees. I got the plane in the air and circled repeatedly to get free of the trees. Eventually, I got above them all and headed due west, straight and level.

    This dream makes me wonder. Am I finally on a path out of the woods? Will I finally be able to fly freely again?

April 12, 2020

This Easter is not unlike the first. We are shut in and isolated "behind locked doors" for fear of the [COVID-19] virus. Like the first disciples, we are all in some ways cut off and at a distance from one another. Still, our circumstances do not mean that God is not here. God raised Jesus from the dead, and no locked doors could keep him away from his friends.

It's on this Easter—for the first time in a very, very long time—that I believe I may finally be on my way to a different kind of resurrection. For the first time in a very long while, the logjam of circumstance and futility may finally be breaking. Perhaps the stone is indeed being rolled away from the tomb of my temporary death and exile.

PRAYERS

July 17, 2015

Lord,

Help me do my best while I am here. Grant me energy and strength for my tasks. Help me model the actions and attributes of Jesus.

When anxiety and fear show up, break their chains! Don't let them take me hostage. When I doubt your care and concern for me, remind me of your love and faithfulness. In all things, even this, let your will be done. Amen.

August 7, 2015

Lord,

I can feel my anxiety rising again.

I feel empty and too flawed and too human to be of use to the church and your kingdom.

I wonder what you're up to—if there's any place I can serve that won't destroy me.

I wonder how to change lives when so much energy and time are spent running the business.

I wonder how this latest chapter will end—will I find productive ministry, or will I leave my calling with a sense of failure and shame? I need an "Abraham" moment—a moment in which you make a future out of barrenness and wandering. I came here with such high hopes—hopes that this place was on the verge of an awakening and a fresh movement of the Spirit. I came with these hopes and many others.

Instead, I'm left wondering if I have a job and a future.

August 30, 2015
Lord,

I truly have no idea how all this is going to end. There is an air of unreality to all of it. Yet here I am doing my work, knowing all the while that an end may be coming, and time is short. Is this like death? For the time being, all I can do is wait and pray. You are all I have. You alone are my hope and strength.

Thank you for a family that loves me and stands with me. Ginny is truly my soul mate—she sees only the best in me. Mary V is an absolute joy and delight.

Lord, this is where I am today. This is not all that is inside me. As best as I can, I trust myself and all that is within me to your good care. Let the path unfold as it should. Amen.

June 15, 2016

Lord, I need you to save me. I need for you to show me the way. I want to make the best use of my gifts. Aside from teaching at McAfee, there is nothing on the horizon. I don't know which way to turn, what to do, or where to search. Please show me the way. Please open a door. Please, Lord, don't let me wither on the vine. I wish to be free of anything that prohibits me from embracing life to the fullest. I have spoken to you countless times and affirmed my openness to anything—whatever your will might be. Why don't you show me? Can I not have something to hold on to? Please have mercy on my soul. Amen.

June 16, 2016

So it is, O Lord, that I come before you in great humility and with abundant gratitude. Please show me your steadfast mercy and loving-kindness by allowing me to find the avenue of service most in keeping with your will. Do not let all that I have sought to do be in vain. Do not let my life vanish in the desert like a mirage. Let me see your power at work in my life. Give me a place of service. Help me see clearly what you wish of me. Let me do your will and let me know that you love me! Honor your promise, O Lord. Amen.

January 19, 2017

Once again, I'm going to use my written words to lay my life before God. These are the questions I'm asking of myself.

Have I allowed God to make the best use of this interim period? Have I been so focused on finding work that I have missed allowing God to work in me and shape my life?

How can I fully surrender? What do I need to let go? How do I allow God to bring life out of this living death?

Lord, help me to release my life into your hands. Amen.

March 11, 2017

The trail I walk in the park in Collegedale has provided much inspiration for my prayers.

The sight of water rushing over the rocks in the creek bed. Today, let your Spirit rush through my life, pushing aside all the debris that clutters my soul.

The sight of deep pools where the water collects before making its headlong rush downhill. Lord, deepen my soul. Let me be as still and centered as those waters.

The sight of a spider web on the covered bridge over the creek. Lord, let me find my place in the web of your kingdom.

The sight of the big bridge over the creek near my turn-around spot. Lord, let my life be a bridge to others. Give me the courage to clear whatever obstacles so that I may show your mercy to others.

The long path itself. Lord, help me remain on your path and to walk it as faithfully as I can. Allow me to enjoy the journey and to welcome other transitions with joy and delight.

As the rising sun begins to illuminate the surrounding hills, Lord, let your light illumine my life and dispel its shadows.

April 1, 2017

For the first time in my life, I put out a "fleece" as Gideon did and received an answer! I had asked God to confirm for me by March 31 if an opportunity I sought was indeed a viable option. Sure enough, yesterday I received a letter stating that I was not selected. While frustrating, it made me aware that God has not lost track of me. I am loved and valued. As well, I told myself that I should be grateful for the doors that have closed. These things, too, are a part of God's direction. Every closed door keeps me on the path to an open door.

February 10, 2018

Lord, I am most grateful for the surgeon who put my ankle back together. I am grateful for the nurses and technicians who have done much to promote my healing. I am grateful for all the friends who have showered me with affection and promises of prayer. I am grateful for my wife and daughter whose love and care know no bounds. These are your good gifts to me. You have blessed me. I offer you my profound gratitude. Amen.

April 25, 2018

Gracious and thoughtful God, I thank you for making it possible for me to be here at Georgetown. Already I feel the stirrings of new life. It seems you have planted me in the midst of some very fine and gifted people. In whatever way possible, let me be a good friend to them. Thank you for these grand and inspiring teachers who have fed my yearning to learn. Amen.

June 22, 2018

My reflections from Mark 4:35-41 and Jesus' determination to "cross to the other side" inspired this prayer.

Merciful God,

I have to cross to the other side: from my shattered confidence to renewed confidence in my calling and my gifts.

I have to cross to the other side: from being pulled apart by anxiety and fear to a place of strong and abiding peace.

I have to cross to the other side: from my shaky and unstable faith to a confident trust in your mercy and purpose.

Whatever it takes, O Lord, help me get to other side. No matter what storms I may encounter along the way, take me to the other side. Amen.

July 9, 2018

Lord, once again another door has closed. The interim I thought I was about to snag fell away. Things are slipping away from me, and the stress is getting to me. Please help me find my way. Amen.

October 31, 2018

God, once again you have come through for us! Thank you for allowing Ginny to get the job she desired. Make full use of her gifts as she ministers in your name. Amen.

November 20, 2018

I passed! Lord, I am so thankful to have completed the last requirement for my coaching certification. The experience has been wonderfully refreshing. Once again, your Spirit has moved to bring goodness into my life. Grateful! Amen.

October 3, 2019

I am sensing some kind of a shift deep within. I feel more at peace despite my anxiety about our long-term future. I know I am weary of worrying. Perhaps the biggest thing I'm sensing is the subtle move from "give me" to "make me" as expressed in the parable of the Prodigal Son. For the last several years, I have hounded God, begging for a new job and a new opportunity. I am beginning to realize that I should be praying "make me" instead of carping about what hasn't shown up yet.

Lord, use my experience to grow into whatever you wish as a result of all the mess I've endured. Amen.

October 20, 2019

Lord, I've had the feeling of late that I no longer know how to pray. My words seem repetitious and hollow. Adding to my distress is the fact that I have begun to doubt whether you are willing and/or able to help me. For the longest time, I have prayed for a job—any kind of job—yet no door opens. I am so frustrated that my gifts are lying dormant. I have so few opportunities to put them to work.

Is this your plan for me?

Is this what my life is coming to?

You have called me to preach, yet recent experience suggests that is all in vain. I have long proclaimed that you care for the individual; yet the evidence of your care for me seems awfully thin! I feel lost to you. Why is it that I cannot find my place? Over the last few years, I have had glimpses of hope. Opportunities seem to be forthcoming. I get excited. Then it all vanishes.

Where are you?

Why do you not grant me this one thing?

Is this too big for you?

In this period of exile, lots of people have told me "the Lord has something special in mind for you." Really? Is that at all true?

How long, O Lord, how long?

Amen.

REFLECTIONS ON JOB

As I mentioned at the outset of this chapter, I have taken refuge in the book of Job during this sojourn in the wilderness. I found comfort in this ancient tale because Job asked many of the questions I was asking. Although my experience was not as grave as his, I did find some significant points of contact that prompted the reflections below. My understanding of Job is limited; I have had to lean on the guidance of others in making my way through the book. In particular, I am indebted to the outstanding Joban scholar J. Gerald Janzen. His book *At the Scent of Water: The Ground of Hope in the Book of Job* was a trustworthy guide and helped me frame many of my ideas.

Job 1:1; 2:1-10, Part 1

First thoughts. Job asks hard questions. Necessary questions.

Right from the beginning, the book raises a question that has tied me in knots throughout my wilderness journey—namely, what does it mean to have faith in God?

The opening chapter recounts a conversation between God and the Adversary. Once God hears that the Adversary has been exploring the world, God jumps at the chance to brag about Job: "Since you have been all over, I bet you couldn't find anyone anywhere who is as righteous as Job!" To which the Adversary shoots back: "Why shouldn't Job be good? Does he serve you for nothing? You have put up a hedge all around his life, protecting him. You shower him with good things. I bet if you take all that away, he'll curse you and turn away from you in a heartbeat!"

Right from the start, the book puts forward a probing question. Do I serve God for nothing? Will I stick with God even if there is no return? If all my blessings were taken away, would I still hang with God? Do I love God for God's sake, or do I love God only for my sake?

I answer by saying that my faith is a mix of the two. I don't think anyone's faith is completely free of some measure of self-interest, and that's certainly true of me. After all, much of what I have shared from my journal entries and prayers reveals how much I have asked from God for myself. During my wandering in the wilderness, I have not been able to get completely out of myself. I have, however, learned one important truth. Although God hasn't come through for me in ways I desperately wanted and my prayers for a new opportunity have yet to be answered, I have remained faithful. I haven't quit God. I can't walk away from my faith, as tenuous as it is these days.

Still, the Adversary's question has forced me to examine the ways faith is proclaimed these days. We are currently saturated with a consumer-driven, transactional approach to faith. If I give God this, God will give me that. If I do this for God, God will do this for me. Faith is about striking a bargain with God. Although I have railed against prosperity preachers who have carried this idea to extremes, I have to acknowledge that many of my prayers have been all about God doing something for me. I am guilty of having a "what's in it for me?" approach to faith. Humbling!

Still, my experience has served me well in that it has corrected much of my praying. Prayer is not just about asking and seeking, nor is it all about being persistent. I have learned that the form of my prayers has as much to say about me and my idea of God as anything else. My prayers reveal both who I am and what I think about God. Yes, I have stuck with the Almighty even though I have abundant reason to abandon the faith. But I have also learned that my prayers too easily slip into self-absorption.

Job 1:1; 2:1-10, Part 2

The book of Job also makes an inquiry into God's nature. Job's struggles and suffering make him wonder who God is and what God is really after. I suppose we all follow Job's lead here when pain and heartache intrude.

To be candid, the picture of God we get from these opening chapters is not at all comforting. It is less than flattering and certainly casts a shadow.

For example, the book of Job creates the impression that God cares very little for human beings. We matter very little to God. Here's the evidence. Twice, the Adversary talks God into running an experiment with Job's life. Let's find out how righteous and faithful he really is. Let's play with his life and mess with him. In this portrayal, Job is little more than a pawn in a celestial poker game, suggesting that God toys with human beings and gambles with their lives.

This exchange between God and the Adversary reminds me of a clip from the film *The Adjustment Bureau*. At the heart of the movie is the assertion is that "the Chairman" has a plan for everyone's life, and we are surrounded by the Chairman's agents—representatives of the Adjustment Bureau—whose task is to keep everyone's life on track and unfolding according to plan. At a pivotal point in the film, the lead agent says, "There is no such thing as free will. Oh yes, you can choose what kind of coffee you'll buy, but beyond that free will is just too risky." That's how God comes off here. We have no say. It's all a plan. We're part of the game, and the game itself is rigged. We're just cogs in the machinery—easily replaced.

Beyond that uncomfortable notion, Job also suggests that God is arbitrary and capricious. In his second exchange with The Adversary, God responds with some of the most troubling words in the book of Job: "[Job] still persists in his integrity, although you incited me against him, to destroy him for no reason" (Job 2:3, NRSV). Not only did God allow himself to be "incited"—trash-talked by the Adversary into destroying Job's life—but God did it for "no reason." By means of this exchange, the book of Job questions God's faithfulness and God's character. God can be talked into something God will later regret. God will act for "no good reason" other than to win a bet.

I find these descriptions disquieting to say the least. After all, Jesus stressed that God is good to all, and God's care is such that not even the falling of a sparrow escapes notice. Jesus also taught that God shows no partiality. It rains on the just and the unjust alike. Blessing comes to all.

Still, I have kept company with Job ever since I descended into the wilderness. I have, for example, questioned God's care and concern for the individual. As my journal entries indicate, I felt forgotten and insignificant the longer I encountered an absence of opportunity. No matter how hard I tried, I couldn't get God's attention. In addition, I wondered about the things that happen "for no reason." Through lots of conversations, Ginny and I have attempted to make sense of things. We never could "connect the dots," and in frustration Ginny has repeatedly exclaimed, "This just makes no sense!" There seemed to be no rhyme or reason for our experience. Thus, I flirted with Job's description of God as arbitrary and capricious.

These ideas are not new, nor are they far from the surface whenever our lives are thrown into upheaval. God doesn't seem to care, and lots of things apparently happen "for no good reason." At such moments, it's easy to question God's faithfulness, power, and love.

Job 2:11-13; 4:1-6

Once word of all the calamities Job had endured reached the ears of his three friends, they hurried to his side to provide what comfort they could. When they finally saw Job, they were astonished by the way suffering had altered his appearance. In response, these three friends mourned with Job and sat with him seven days and seven nights in silence.

At the end of the book, these three friends do not fare well. The Lord takes them to task for the way they have misrepresented the Almighty (Job 42:7). Their explanation of how and why suffering occurs does not accurately represent God's ways.

Still, let's give them some credit. When they heard of Job's trouble, they rushed to his side. They mourned with Job. Most important, they simply sat with Job and kept silence for seven days and nights. Those are the gestures good friends typically offer. I will elaborate more on the roles my friends have played in my life in the next chapter. For the time being, however, let me say that my truest friends grieved with me and offered me the gift of their presence. They checked on me regularly. They prayed when I needed prayer. They laughed with me when I called attention to the absurdity of stuff. They allowed me room and space to cuss and vent my anger. Timely help!

The counsel of Job's friends was ineffective because it was unimaginative and reflected the conventional thinking of the day: suffering equals sin. The notion that God rewards the faithful with blessing but punishes the wicked with suffering and trouble is one of the threads running through the entire book. Fortunately, none of my friends bought into that equation regarding my life. Still, many, although they were well meaning and certainly had my best interests at heart, attempted to comfort me by citing the conventional wisdom that is so much a part of popular theology. Time and again, I was told that "God has a plan" or "God is in control." Many friends also attempted to reassure me that I wasn't done by frequently declaring, "The Lord must be getting you ready for something really special."

While I certainly appreciated my friends' attempts to offer hope and comfort, I was not entirely comfortable with their conventional theological wisdom. Take, for instance, the assertion that "God has a plan." I think I know what they meant by that. This well-worn phrase offers the assurance that God is continually working, and one day, all the pieces will come together in glorious fashion. That certainly offers a measure of hope. Nevertheless, if God has a plan, then why do some suffer and never find any resolution? If God has a plan, why do some thrive while others encounter nothing but misery?

Similarly, the catchphrase "God is in control" troubled me. What exactly does that mean? That God micromanages the universe? That nothing happens unless God wills it? Such affirmations tread awfully close to making God the author of both good *and* evil, something Jesus refused to countenance.[17] To honor my friends, I put my own spin on this theological shibboleth, taking it as an affirmation that God works to keep the waters of chaos at bay and as a reminder that God does indeed have a lot to answer for.

Instead of affirming God's control, I find it more palatable to assert that God is at work. The whole of Scripture, from Genesis to Revelation, bears consistent witness to this idea. "In the beginning, God created" leads ultimately to "Behold! I am making all things new!" Instead of controlling everything that happens, God works within what happens—taking the raw material of broken life to create something new.

Terence Fretheim's observation that God created the world "good but not perfect" reinforces this conclusion.[18] Creation, Fretheim says, is not tightly woven silk; instead, it is more like burlap.[19] There's some give in the created order, and that give allows space for whatever is bad or random or arbitrary to intrude into human life. But that same loose weave also gives God space to work and to exercise the divine capacity for endless and imaginative creative work.

Last, the hopeful affirmation that "The Lord must be getting you ready for something really special" doesn't work. To be candid, when I hear that, I almost always conclude that I must be a terribly slow learner if it's taken me this long to get ready! Again, this piece of encouragement is well intended. It is no doubt grounded in Paul's affirmation that "in all things God works for good for those who love him and are called according to his purpose."[20] Hopefully what I have experienced will eventually be shown to have been hemmed by God's goodness. I harbor the stubborn hope that whenever this season ends, many of the rough and jagged pieces of my life will fit together in such a way that I can celebrate God's creativity. The long wait, however, does not necessarily mean that some larger-than-life opportunity is looming down the road. The length of one's sojourn in the wilderness does not automatically translate into a heightened opportunity. Somewhere along the line I came across this pithy little saying: "things take longer than things take." As God works with all the variables present in a planet inhabited by 7.5 billion people, things do take longer than things take!

Job 23:1-10, 16-17

In this chapter, Job finally gets what he wants: his day in court. Job wants to present his case and plead his innocence. Job wants God to meet him in the courtroom so he can present his evidence to the Almighty. "I have done nothing wrong. You've made a terrible mistake inflicting all this suffering on me! You've got the wrong man; I'm innocent!" Job reasoned that if he could get God in court, he could get some relief.

This approach was the very opposite of what his so-called friend, Eliphaz, counseled. In the preceding chapter, Eliphaz had argued for the umpteenth time that the extent of Job's suffering meant he had surely done something terribly wrong. He was suffering because he had sinned. Eliphaz urged Job to swallow his pride and submit: "Agree with God and be at peace; in this way good will come to you." Admit your sin, keep quiet, and all will be well. Job would have none of that and exclaims at the outset of the chapter, "Today also my complaint is rebellious; my hand is heavy despite my groaning" (Job 23:2, NRSV).

Submit? No way! Agree? Not going to happen! Keep quiet? Forget that! Job rebelled against Eliphaz's counsel and rejected it out of hand! On this score, Job is less than the patient Job we often speak about and is instead the impatient Job! He's had enough! He's worn himself out praying and can barely raise his hands in prayer. He wants a court date. He is convinced God will hear and answer his arguments. He is convinced God will show restraint in dealing with him. He is convinced that, when all the evidence is on the table, God will acquit him. All he had to do is get God to show up in court.

But that was the real problem for Job. He couldn't find God. He couldn't find God anywhere: "If I go forward, he is not there; or backward, I cannot perceive him; on the left he hides, and I cannot behold him; I turn to the right but, I cannot see him" (Job 23:8-9, NRSV). He had looked for God in every direction—north, south, east, and west— and God was nowhere to be found. He couldn't find God or see God. In the face of his persistent prayer, heaven remained silent. Job was waiting in the courtroom, legal pads and briefs at the ready, but God never showed. All Job got for his trouble was silence and empty space. All he got for his trouble was—nothing!

This sense of God's absence or silence is one of the things we don't talk much about. Popular portrayals of faith promise a miracle a minute and continuous victory. But the truth is, faith often has its moments of darkness. When that happens, our prayers get stale and feel like nothing more than words thrown up into empty space. Scripture can lose its edge, and its words can fall flat. God doesn't seem real or close. These are not new experiences; people of faith everywhere and at all times have known such moments.

Like Job, I ran head-on into the fact that for all our talk of God's love and God's presence, God can be awfully hard to find. Although I searched in every direction, I found no trace. The Lord remained hidden. The hard truth is that the God we love and serve reveals and conceals at the same time. While God reveals, God also remains hidden.

As disturbing as this portrayal is, Job is my hero! Confronted by God's silence and absence, Job does the one thing, the only thing, he can do: he refuses to remain quiet! Take a look at the last two verses in this chapter. I like the way the Revised English Bible renders them: "It is God who makes me faint-hearted, the Almighty who fills me with fear, yet I am not reduced to silence by the darkness or by the mystery which hides him" (Job 23:16-17). In the face of God's silence and the accompanying darkness, Job refused to back down and keep quiet. Job shouted! If God remains absent and silent, then Job is going to fill the void with words. He will speak his pain, his innocence, and his disappointment with God.

This is not the way we have been taught to speak with God, is it? We have learned to offer our thanks and praise. We have learned the language of confession and contrition. We have learned to ask God for guidance and direction. These, it seems to me, are our usual ways of speaking to God.

But Job shows us that when confronted with God's silence, there is one other, perhaps healthier, way of speaking. Job will let his pain speak. He will call on God to do right. He will protest at the top of his lungs and will keep on until his voice gives out. He will shout. He refuses to remain silent and let God off the hook.

I imagine this reaction does not come easily to us, but there is ample precedent for it in Scripture. The prophet Jeremiah, for example, agonized over the fact that he was "called to preach but condemned to survive."[21] He preached his heart out, and nothing changed. When he was persecuted for doing the very thing God called him to do, Jeremiah cried out to God: "You seduced me! You overpowered me and made me do this!"[22] As well, Jesus did not go quietly into the darkness of death. In his agony on the cross, he called out to God, "My God, My God, why have you forsaken me?" (Mark 15:34, NRSV).

As uncomfortable as that is, it's awfully close to the tone of Job's argument here. Job will not be reduced to silence. And the really beautiful thing about Job's rant is that God prefers Job's outrage and demands to the speeches of Job's friends! Their speeches are nothing but pious platitudes. When we're in pain and when God remains in hiding, we are free to yell as loudly as we wish. I will not be reduced to silence. Even when everything goes dark and even when my cries are greeted with silence, I will not give up on God. I will keep speaking my heart and my mind. I will not be reduced to silence. "Devout defiance pleases God. It may even bring God out of hiding . . . ."[23]

Job 38:1-7

After Job's many, many calls for God to meet him, for God to show up in court so he could make his case, for God to break the silence, God finally speaks: "The LORD answered Job out of the whirlwind." God then proceeds to give Job an earful. Once God gets started, he doesn't stop. God answers Job out of the whirlwind with a barrage of questions. Who are you? Where were you? Are you able? One question after another in rapid succession. God goes on like that for 123 verses. Once God gets started, Job doesn't have much of chance to respond.

No wonder the writer of this fascinating book said God spoke to Job "out of the whirlwind." All those questions set Job spinning. Job had pleaded with God to show up, and when God did, there was a storm of words. In this respect, Scripture frequently portrays God speaking through the elements of a great storm. It's a common image. The psalmist, for example, put it this way: "He came swiftly upon the wings of the wind.... The LORD also thundered in the heavens, and the Most High uttered his voice. And he sent out his arrows, and scattered them; he flashed forth lightnings, and routed them" (Ps 18:10, 13-15, NRSV). Similar examples are found in Psalm 29:3 and Nahum 1:3. Naturally, the images of whirlwind and storm convey great power. We readily understand that. A whirlwind signals power, the kind of power that makes our knees weak and our spirits wither.

By speaking to Job through the megaphone of a whirlwind, God humbled Job and impressed him with his power. The whole point of this divine bombardment, many say, was to make Job feel small: "See, I am of small account; what shall I answer you?"

But if that's all there is to God's answer, it's really not much of an answer at all. Missing from this inspiring demonstration of power is God's answer to the questions that troubled Job the most. Why do the innocent suffer? Why do bad things happen to good people? How can God allow such things to occur? What about all those things that happen for "no reason"?

These are the questions Job raises from the ash heap. These are the questions he poses while scraping his broken flesh with shards of shattered pottery. These are the questions that remain unanswered. And yes, these are the questions drowned out by the sound of God's howling voice.

Thankfully, there's more to it than that. There has to be, or we're all sunk! Gerald Janzen has suggested that the whirlwind is not only a sign of power but also a sign of hope and life. To make his point, he quotes an old Palestinian proverb: "The east wind awakens the west wind."[24] In the summer, the east wind is hot and dry, and it scorches the earth. In the fall, however, the east wind works in such a way as to prompt the rise of the west wind, the wind that brings rain and renewal.[25] God answers Job out of the whirlwind, and this swirling wind is a harbinger of life! The whirlwind from which God speaks carries the scent of water and with it the hope that death and suffering are no match for the power of life. The whirlwind out of which God speaks invites us to walk in God's world and open our eyes to its wonder so that we, too, may join in the song of the morning stars.

Although God has not spoken to me out of a whirlwind, I do know that my sojourn in the wilderness has humbled me. I still have lots of questions for which I may never get a satisfactory answer. Yet, throughout this hard season, I have been reminded time and again that I am flesh and blood. I was raised from the dust, and someday I'll return to dust. In the meantime, however, God's west wind has blown through this ordeal, and I have caught the scent of water, thirsting with good reason to keep on hoping in God.

Job 40:6–41:34

After giving Job a grand tour of the created order, God takes a breath and gives Job a chance to respond. Job speaks briefly, acknowledging that he is so very small in the grand scheme of things. He has no words to offer in return. He is speechless.

At that point, God speaks to Job for a second time out of the whirlwind. Once again God seeks to humble Job. God tells Job to "buckle up"; God isn't through with Job yet! At first glance, I concluded that God was piling on—hadn't Job been humbled enough already? It's one thing to humble someone; it's quite another to humiliate them. The picture that came to mind is that God was rubbing Job's nose in it.

I was alerted, however, to the fact that God's speaking strikes a hopeful note. God answers Job not once but twice!

God's twofold response underscores God's care for the suffering.[26] Despite the witness of our experience, God *does* hear us and takes note of our struggles.

My sojourn in the wilderness frequently led me to question whether God knew I was alive. As is evident in the journal entries and prayers in this chapter, I repeatedly wondered if God had forgotten me. I was at odds with Jesus' insistence that God cares for the lowliest sparrow and is able to number all the hairs on our heads. I have had many moments when I wondered if God knew my name. In hindsight, I can see that God has indeed attended to my prayers. God has answered me, maybe not as I wished but certainly in a manner that demonstrated that I was not forgotten.

That's not the only hopeful word this part of Job offers. Beginning in 40:15 and ending at 41:34, God calls attention to two creatures, Behemoth and Leviathan. God describes the creatures in great detail and stresses their power. Tony Cartledge playfully likens them to "Godzilla" and the "Loch Ness monster."[27] There is, however, much scholarly debate over the role of these two creatures in God's second address to Job.[28] In the face of that extensive conversation, I offer my own conclusion. Behemoth and Leviathan are symbols of the powers and the chaos that threaten humankind. No one (Job included!) except God is up to the task of holding them in check.[29] Implied in this lengthy description is something I have leaned on. God keeps these powers at bay in ways no one can see or fathom. We don't see exactly how God restrains these powers; we do, however, benefit from this hidden exercise of God's power.

Throughout my wilderness journey, I have leaned hard on what I have come to call God's "dark presence." God has indeed been at work in my life, but I have not always seen it firsthand. I have been carried in ways I did not know. "The hidden hand of God" has been at work beneath the circumstances of my life.[30]

Here are a few examples. In this and preceding chapters, I have mentioned the number of opportunities that seemed to beckon only to be snatched away. Those moments have certainly been frustrating, and I have lamented my inability to land a job somewhere. Yet how would I have managed without those fleeting opportunities? What if nothing had come my way? If that had indeed been the case, I am certain despair would have overtaken me. I can't tell for sure at this moment, but I have begun to think that those periodic glimpses of new possibilities have enabled me to keep moving and not give up. I have been given enough hope to keep on.

As well, I suspect that God's dark presence has saved me *from* some things that would have unleashed more chaos in my life.[31] I have learned yet again that providence is not solely about doors opening; it also encompasses doors that remain closed. Hindrance is also a form of God's guidance and direction.

Finally, my experience of dark presence mirrors an overlooked aspect of God's character, particularly with regard to providence. My former professor, mentor, and friend, Dr. Frank Tupper, introduced me to the idea of God's self-limitation. As he put it, the traditional affirmation of God as all-powerful has to be qualified. God, in order to grant life and freedom to human beings, has to limit God's self. Thus, God has chosen to work *within* the structures of human circumstance and the nexus of human relationships as opposed to overpowering them and imposing on them from *without*. For example, God defeated death by experiencing it fully through the son, Jesus Christ. God accomplished this by working from within the confines of death itself. In this way, Jesus reveals that God's providence is an *embodied providence* at work within the limits of human experience. As a result, in any given situation, God works with all the complex variables life presents and does all that God can do.[32] Similarly, Tupper also stressed that although circumstances may be random and arbitrary, God is not![33]

In this light, God does indeed hold Behemoth and Leviathan in check, but despite God's best efforts, chaos catches up with us. Within the boundaries God has set for God's self, God is always doing all God can. Yes, my life has been invaded by the forces of chaos. I have felt the keen edge of the arbitrary. Still, I believe God is good and not arbitrary. Even though God has not come through in ways I wished or hoped, God is still at work, doing all God can to bring blessing into my life.

Job 42:1-6, 10-17

Some creative confusion shows up at the conclusion of the book of Job. For centuries, many have argued that the book rightfully concludes with Job's final speech. Throughout his ordeal, Job has railed at God. He has demanded a face-to-face meeting. He wants an explanation for his trouble. God appears in a whirlwind and brushes aside all of Job's questions. When Job finally gets to respond, all he can muster are words of contrition: "I have uttered what I did not understand, things too wonderful for me, which I did not know. . . . I had heard of you by the hearing of the ear, but now my eye sees you, therefore I despise myself and repent" (Job 42:3, NRSV).

In many ways, this seems like an appropriate conclusion. Everything is put back in place. God is exalted; Job is humbled. There are no easy answers given to the painful questions that have been raised. Ending the book with Job's final speech reflects the way life works for most of us. You know and I know that life has rough edges. Good and neat endings do not always occur. Issues are not always resolved in twenty-five minutes as they are on TV sitcoms. There are no easily packaged answers to the dilemmas we face. All too often, life leaves us where Job was. All we can say is, "I don't understand. There's a lot that's beyond me." To be sure, that's not the kind of ending we want, but sometimes it's the ending we get.

Somewhere along the way, however, a good ending was tacked on to Job's story. The conclusion sounds remarkably like a fairy tale; it possesses a "they lived happily ever after" quality. In the epilogue, Job gets back everything he lost twice over. He recovers his place in the community. He regains his family. He accumulates great wealth. He has ten more children and lives to see his great-grandchildren. Job lives a long life and dies, "sated with days." Cue the music—a swelling crescendo. Throw up the words "The End" and roll the credits. That's the kind of ending we like, isn't it? We would like to think that the good things we enjoy and the evil we suffer will eventually balance out and tilt toward the good. We would like to think that whenever we suffer, we get back everything we lose and then some. That's comforting, but I don't think it always happens.

Instead, the good ending underscores the fact that Job resumes his life to the fullest. He welcomes his family. He and his wife enlarge their brood. His cattle business thrives. Why is that so striking? *For Job to resume life in this way is to risk losing it all again!* In the face of what he has already lost, Job is willing to risk living again.[34]

That's not easy—not at all. I have known couples who have risked having a child when they have already lost a child. That takes a lot of courage! The ending also makes clear that Job embraced his wife even though she offered him little support in his trials. It takes a stout soul to forgive and start over when the one we love has let us down. But Job, in the face of all he has lost, is willing to risk losing it again just for one more chance to live, to embrace life to the fullest.

This ending is a good ending—and not because everything turns out just right for Job. This is a good ending because Job recognizes that despite all his suffering and God's long silence, God did indeed remember him. This is a good ending because it affirms God's intention to redeem our suffering. And this is a good ending because Job, after having come so near death, is willing to live again. There is a statement in the Talmud, the collected wisdom of the rabbis from the first five centuries, that I have always found striking. It goes like this: "In the world to come, each of us will be called to account for all the good things God put on earth which we refused to enjoy."[35] If Job teaches us anything, it's that our losses don't have the final say about the ending of our story.

This tacked-on happy ending has confronted me with a difficult question: would I be willing to reenter ministry and risk enduring another hard experience? I can't answer that question until the possibility presents itself. That said, the ending of Job has afforded me much comfort and encouragement. No, I don't think I'll regain everything I've lost. But, as I mentioned above, this ending gives me great hope that my losses will not have the final say. The wilderness will not be my home forever.

CONCLUDING REFLECTIONS

Times of testing reveal the character of our faith. Difficulty exposes the faulty assumptions undergirding our efforts to know and walk with God. At the same time, our season in the wilderness uncovers the most genuine aspects of our trust in the Almighty. Making our way through inhospitable territory makes us aware of what stands in need of correction and also gives us reason to rejoice in what is firm and true.

Our prayers reveal what we truly think and believe about God. Most certainly, our prayers lay bare our understanding of providence and God's way of working in the world. When our ideas about God's work in the world collide with unyielding reality, the only choice we have is to recalibrate our understanding. Honesty and forthrightness are essential if we are to find our way to a new understanding. Uncomfortable but gritty prayers are often the best expression of a living relationship with God.

My record of events and my prayers in this chapter reveal that life is not always on an upward arc. We regularly swing between highs and lows. One moment we're hopeful, and the next we feel bereft and abandoned. Many of our biblical heroes oscillated between courage and fear. Abraham comes to mind, as does King David. Peter certainly manifested this tendency. Going up the mountain and descending into the valley are part and parcel of our faith experience.

We have no idea how the decisions we make will play out over time. Our line of sight is very, very limited. Despite our well-designed plans and our best preparation, life sometimes carries us to unexpected destinations.

Conventional wisdom, though well intended, may not always be helpful. Popular theology dressed in the garb of pithy clichés may work on a bumper sticker, but it doesn't capture the complexity of human life. Although we may be at odds with the words our friends offer, we must listen for the love and care that prompted those words in the first place. Better to rejoice that some have chosen to sit with us than to pick an argument.

Scripture is a vital companion whenever we are plunged into the wilderness. Reading the stories of our forebears in faith and chewing on the questions they raised remind us that we are not alone in our struggle. Our forebears asked the questions we ask. They struggled to keep faith when they encountered difficulty and wandered in the wilderness. Their prayers help us find our voice when we don't know what to say to God.

I remain firmly committed to God. Over the last several years, chaos has played with my life. My faith has been tested and tried in ways I never imagined. God has given me enough hope to keep going, managing one chapter of life's story at a time. Although God hasn't come through for me in the ways I hoped, I still can't quit God. If anything, faith is nothing but perseverance. Like Job's did for him, my experience has sifted my soul. And like Job, I have begun to learn the difference between desiring God's blessings and simply longing for God alone.

QUESTIONS FOR REFLECTION

1. What spiritual disciplines do you practice? Have they been helpful to you in hard times? If so, how?

2. What is the normal temper and tone of your prayers? Do your prayers truly reflect what's inside you?

3. Identify the Scriptures you turn to in moments of difficulty. Why do you gravitate to those texts? Have they remained consistently helpful?

4. How do you understand God's providence? How does God work in this world and in your life?

5. How do you understand God's part and your part in achieving God's purpose?

CHAPTER 4

SUSTAINED

I will make a way in the wilderness and rivers in the desert.
—Isaiah 43:19b

I want to know if you can see Beauty even when it is not pretty every day. And if you can source your own life from its presence.
—Oriah Mountain Dreamer[36]

The preceding chapters reveal that my sojourn in the wilderness was hard. The longer I resided in that difficult place, the more questions I had. I questioned God. I wondered if God was indeed able to save. I questioned myself, my call, and my place in God's kingdom. Many times I was terribly frustrated and angry. Because there seemed to be no end or resolution in sight, there were times I broke down and wept. The wilderness was unyielding and relentless, and it very nearly got the best of me.

Nevertheless, I do not wish to leave the impression that I found nothing but emptiness and desolation there. Like so many who have traveled endless stretches of desert, I found oases, places where I slaked my thirst and renewed my strength. In short, at different points along the way, I was sustained. I was given enough to keep going, enough to wake up every day and keep putting one foot in front of the other.

Scripture bears ample witness to the ways in which God sustained people and kept them alive. The writer of Exodus, for example, recalled a time when God's people complained to Moses. They had no water and were afraid they would shrivel and die. To counter this threat, God provided. God commanded Moses to strike the rock at the base of Mt. Horeb, and when he did, water gushed out (see Exod 17:1-7). In similar and surprising fashion, God kept the prophet Elijah alive during a season of famine. When Elijah camped out by the Wadi Cherinth, God kept him alive by sending ravens with food, and he drank from the wadi until its waters ceased. When those sources ran out, God sent Elijah to the home of a widow who had just enough for one last meal for herself and her son. God used this unlikely figure to sustain the prophet. As long as he remained in her house, there was plenty to eat (see 1 Kings 17). The prophet Isaiah relayed God's promise to the people of Israel returning home from exile. Although their journey would take them through inhospitable places, Isaiah promised they would find "streams in the desert" (Isa 35:5-6). Finally, at the conclusion of Jesus' temptation, Mark tells us that "the angels waited on him" (Mark 1:13). The word Mark used here suggests that they brought him food.[37] The angels, as God's messengers, represented God's presence, reminding Jesus that he was not forgotten or abandoned. Taken together, these Scriptures vividly portray God's sustaining grace.

Once again, I must lean on the insights of Frank Tupper, who, in his work on the providence of God, thoughtfully described God's sustaining grace. To do so, he drew a careful distinction between "healing" grace and "sustaining" grace.[38] Healing grace, according to Tupper, affirms that a door to deliverance may indeed swing open. In some instances, healing may be a live possibility. When no such door exists and no such door can be created, however, God may make available a "window of sustaining grace."[39] Sustaining grace may enable continued transformation amid hardship and may also provide the resources to cope and survive. My wife Ginny put her own spin on it when she commented, "When I got to my lowest point, God was still with me, and that was enough. It was barely enough, but it was enough." Sustaining grace keeps us alive, and, in Isaiah's words, it affords us the daily strength to "walk and not faint" (Isa 40:31c, NRSV).

The witness I offer in the following pages adheres to these thoughtful distinctions. For the longest time, no doors of deliverance opened. Try as I might, I couldn't regain my footing long enough to find a way forward. Yet I can testify that in many, many ways I have experienced God's sustaining grace. God has kept me alive in many ways throughout this ordeal, and in the pages that follow, I'd like to describe some of them.

BEING SAVED "FROM"

The churches I have served have typically asked candidates for leadership positions or ordination to offer a testimony to the congregation. For the most part, those testimonies, while genuine and authentic, usually focused on the past. Often, someone would relate their experience of being reared in a Christian home and give a recitation of the events leading up to their profession of faith. I enjoyed hearing those stories and welcomed the glimpse into another person's spirit. Still, these stories had a "long-ago and faraway" quality to them, as though God's activity in the person's life was solely a past event. From time to time, I tried to nudge people into giving an up-to-date testimony by posing a couple of different questions: How has God saved you in the last year? How is God saving you now? I hoped these questions would give people pause and encourage them to reflect on what God was up to in the here and now.

Now it's my turn to answer the questions I asked of others. God has sustained me, and God has been at work in my life throughout this portion of my journey by "saving me from" things that could have been detrimental to me and others. I alluded to this experience in the previous chapter, but I'd like to describe it more fully here.

In the aftermath of stepping away, I assumed I would be able to step back into the pastorate after a hiatus of a year or so. I was so confident of this that I began making inquiries about open pulpits early on. In a couple of instances, I put my name forward and received a church's profile in return. This was exciting. Once I began digesting the contents of a church's profile, I experienced something unexpected: a profound sense of dread. My enthusiasm was short-lived, and the emotions of my most recent negative experience resurfaced with a vengeance. Although I had a conversation or two with some churches, I was almost relieved to hear I hadn't made the cut. I realized that I was nowhere close to being healed and way too fragile to reenter the rough and tumble world of congregational life just yet. If I had, I likely would have done more harm than good, both to the church and to myself. If I had, the residue of my most recent experience would have hindered my efforts to provide leadership. Bottom line: I was saved from these possibilities to allow more time for healing.

As another example, one opportunity I came across would have involved working with aspiring ministers to further their training and development. This prospect excited me tremendously for a couple of reasons. One, I was in that phase of life where "generativity" takes center stage. Passing on the lessons and wisdom experience had imparted to me would be helpful to others and would no doubt have helped me come full circle in terms of my calling. I would have derived immense satisfaction from watching others grow into their gifts and serve God's kingdom. And in conjunction with this work, I would have been able to preach more regularly as an interim or as a supply preacher. This possibility looked like a winner from every vantage point save one: this job would require our family to relocate to a place where we had virtually no connections. The distance between us and our extended families would have increased significantly. Still, if that's what it took, we were ready to go. Once again, however, after submitting an application and the required materials, I learned that I would not be considered. Naturally, I was disappointed. Several months later, I was astonished to learn that the school was likely to close, and the position I had sought would have turned to ashes. To make a move of such consequence only to have it all vanish would have been devastating. Bottom line: I was saved from enormous upheaval.

Here's one final example. During our last year in Dalton, Ginny began participating in the two-year Academy for Spiritual Formation sponsored by The Upper Room. This program required extensive reading and periodic retreats with her cohort. It was an extraordinarily rich experience for her, and as a result, her sense of call reawakened. She paid close attention to the Spirit's promptings and took advantage of any and every opportunity that might help her gain some clarity. With each step, the picture came into focus for her. The result was a renewed interest in chaplaincy.

During her tenure as the campus minister at Samford University, she had taken a basic unit of clinical pastoral education, and that experience was transformative for her. It both deepened her self-awareness and altered her approach to ministry. Years later, that experience found new expression as she determined that the best way forward was for her to apply for a clinical pastoral residency to further her training. The rightness of this step was confirmed while we were on the way home from an interview for an interim position. The interview had gone well, but as the interview progressed, Ginny picked up on a drop in my energy. In the space of an hour or so, she went from thinking "He's back!" to concluding "Not yet!" I was not yet ready for such a responsibility. To help us sort things out, we called Julie, our spiritual director, to talk through this latest development. She listened intently as we described what had transpired. Her immediate response? "What about Ginny? If you take this interim, will Ginny be able to take the next step in fulfilling her calling?" That single question, in tandem with my lack of readiness, confirmed our next steps. Ginny and I decided that her newly awakened sense of call should take priority. She began exploring different avenues and was drawn to pursuing the chaplaincy. Shortly thereafter, Ginny applied and was accepted into the chaplain residency program at Erlanger Hospital in Chattanooga.[40] The training she received there eventually opened a new door of ministry for her as a hospice chaplain. If I had said "yes" to my opportunity, Ginny might have had to say "no" to hers. Bottom line: we were saved from the postponement of Ginny's growth and development as a minister in her own right.

Through these "saved from" events, God's sustaining grace made me aware of my lack of readiness to reenter the ministry. That same grace confirmed Ginny's readiness to embrace her calling more fully.

FRIENDS

The story of Jesus' healing of a paralytic in Mark 2:1-12 offers a portrait of faithful friendship. As such, the episode illustrates the role my friends have played in keeping my soul alive.

In Mark's telling, Jesus had returned home to Capernaum. When the word got out that he had returned, a great crowd gathered around him. His house was filled to overflowing, and those who couldn't get in congregated around the house, hoping to see through an open window what he might do or hear what he might say. Four men bearing a paralyzed man on a stretcher suddenly showed up, hoping to bring their friend to Jesus. Typical of Mark, these four men are never named, and they never say a word. Mark does, however, tell us what they *did*. They *carried* their friend on a stretcher, they *climbed* up to the roof, they *dug* a hole in the roof, and they *lowered* their friend down to Jesus. All the action adds up to something very important. Through their determined actions, these four demonstrated the kind of grit and resolve, the kind of "I won't let anything stop me" quality that Mark identifies as faith.[41] Remarkably, their faith was the catalyst for Jesus' healing activity: "When Jesus saw *their* faith . . ." (Mark 2:5a). Their refusal to stop at nothing to get their friend to Jesus resulted in the forgiveness of his sin and his subsequent healing. Because of their stubborn determination, the paralytic's nerves and muscles came back online and hummed with life. He got up, picked up the mat that had cradled him for so long, and walked out!

I recognize something of the paralytic in me. When I look at him, I see something of the ways my wilderness experience marked me. When I broke my right ankle in three places in 2018, I couldn't put any weight on that foot for nearly four months. The injury effectively immobilized me, and I couldn't get around by myself. I needed help to do almost everything. Although my experience does not nearly approximate that of people who have been paralyzed, I did have a taste of what it is like to be unable to move. If I wanted to go anywhere or do anything, a friend or family member had to make it happen.

On another level, however, I identify to some degree with the paralytic in the story. Like him, I had a hard time getting to God, and on countless occasions my faith seemed as thin as gossamer—absolutely incapable of holding me up. Many people, by their prayers, encouragement, and presence, have kept faith for me when I couldn't. They have shouldered the dead weight of my faith when it bordered on collapse.

My friends thus became for me a sort of "embodied providence," truly reflective of the ways in which human and divine activity intertwine. On more than one occasion, their care spoke to me and reminded me that I was not lost to God.

To illustrate how my friends kept me before God and God before me, I will name four of my "stretcher bearers." In doing so, I in no way wish to diminish or minimize the help others extended. Instead, I wish to call attention to the unique but representative gifts each person offered, gifts that were essential for me to be able to keep going and to keep looking for a way through the wilderness.

I begin with my friend since seminary, Jerry Mantooth. Jerry and I met during our first semester at Southern Seminary, and we have been extremely close ever since. Across the years, we have shared many significant events. When Jerry and Kim got married, I was honored to be one of his groomsmen. Later, I rejoiced with them when they welcomed their daughters, Emily and Ellen, into this world. I was even Emily's first babysitter! When my dad died unexpectedly, Jerry made the long trip from east Tennessee to Mississippi to stand with me during an extraordinarily difficult time. He helped me absorb the loss. Years later, when Ginny and I were married, Jerry was one of the officiants who tied the knot for us. Together we have shared tons of eye-watering laughter and had many rewarding conversations over the years. And, as I noted previously, I turned to Jerry to help me sort out my options when I was in the thick of it at Dalton.

Upon reflection, I realized that Jerry has repeatedly offered me the same gift in many guises. Jerry has always known how to show up and be there. Few people are centered enough to know how to be present without being intrusive. Few people possess the kind of self-awareness it takes to be present without projecting their own agenda. Jerry has the gift of *faithful presence*, and by extending that gift to me, he reminded me that I was not alone.

My second stretcher-bearer was Tim Owings. I knew of Tim from my days at Southern even though he finished his PhD a few years ahead of me. Our paths eventually crossed when we were both serving in Georgia in the early 1990s. That's when I discovered that Tim possessed a boatload of gifts: he was a gifted preacher, an insightful writer, and an incredible musician. He modeled what a good pastor should be and do. Somewhere along the line, we made a connection, and sporadic conversations morphed into a strong friendship.

Despite a successful run as the pastor of several significant churches, Tim had also made the difficult decision to walk away from the pastorate. Thus, when I was pondering the same course of action, he offered a deep understanding both of what I was going through and what I felt. Tim frequently checked in during some of the worst of it and has continued to do so since. His manner during our conversations and the questions he asked showed me that he understood. He had been there and knew what the trail looked like. When one is traversing unfamiliar territory, it's always good to have someone who has been there and understands the terrain. In this respect, Tim offered me the gift of *heartfelt understanding*.

Stephen Cook held up the third corner of my stretcher. When I became the pastor at Ardmore Baptist Church in Winston-Salem, Stephen was already on staff there as a youth minister. Stephen left near the end of my first year to pursue seminary training and fulfill his calling as a pastor. Since then, I have followed his career with great interest and quietly cheered from the sidelines as he has ministered effectively in a number of churches. Despite the difference in our ages and the distance between us, Stephen and I have a strong and lasting friendship.

Once my decision to leave the pastorate became widely known, Stephen was one of the first to contact me, and as my days away from the ministry lengthened into years, he never forgot me. I never fell off his radar. He checked in on me regularly, and we spent hours on the phone together. Stephen's quick wit peppered our conversations, and he simply made me laugh! The laughter we shared created a healthy distance between myself and the things that had happened so that, instead of bemoaning my fate, I was able to laugh at the absurdity that characterized so many of my days. Stephen's lightheartedness kept me from taking myself too seriously. The Wisdom writer had people like Stephen in mind when he offered this observation: "A cheerful heart is good medicine, but a downcast spirit dries up the bones" (Prov 17:22, NRSV). *Wise humor* is as essential to life as food and water. Stephen's ability to get me to laugh at myself was good medicine, and the laughter we shared kept my bones from drying up.

Last but not least among the four is my longtime friend, Randy Hankins. Randy and I met and became friends during the fall of our freshman year at Mississippi College. We connected at a deep level, and for the remainder of our time at MC we were virtually inseparable. Once we graduated, Randy remained in Mississippi to fulfill his ambition to be a primary care physician, a vocation he has embraced and honored for many years. Although distance and responsibilities have made our reunions infrequent, we have always been able to pick things up as though we were next door—a sure sign of a strong friendship!

One of Randy's best gifts is his uncanny ability to see what a situation requires (surely an essential for a good doctor!). His insight is wonderfully married to a generous spirit. When I called early on to let him know what was transpiring in my life, he listened thoughtfully and then responded as he always has over the years: "How can I help? What do you need?" I assured him that we had made a plan in advance of our decision and were fine. Still, he persisted: "That's good. But the offer's still on the table; just let me know." Eventually the day came when I had to take him up on his offer. Going without work for four years had dented our financial reserves, and the medical bills resulting from my broken ankle were significant. Some other things had piled up, and I needed help. I called Randy, fearful of putting him on the spot and making him uncomfortable. He heard me out and responded without hesitation and without judgment: "What do you need?" When I answered, he didn't blink an eye and came through for us not once but twice. He assured me that the opportunity to help gave him a great deal of joy and delight. Randy's *thoughtful generosity* enabled my family to make it through a moment when we were stretched thin.

Four friends. Four distinct and necessary gifts: faithful presence, heartfelt understanding, wise humor, and thoughtful generosity. These offerings kept me sane, alive, and human. Each of these friends carried me, and their faith in God enabled me to stand upright and keep walking. By shouldering the weight of my trouble, they reminded me of an age-old truth summed up beautifully in a poem by Maya Angelou:

> Lying, thinking
> Last night

> How to find my soul a home
> Where water is not thirsty
> And bread loaf is not stone
> I came up with one thing
> And I don't believe I'm wrong
> That nobody,
> But nobody
> Can make it out here alone.[42]

I couldn't have made it this far by myself or in my own strength. All of my friends, as represented in the four I've named, made sure that I was never, ever alone.

My experience has taught me that lasting friendships are one of God's best gifts to us. I hope that my account of the role my friends played will encourage you to tell your friends how grateful you are for their presence in your life. Take time to express your appreciation. At the very least, ask yourself how you can be a better friend to those within your circle. If you lack sustaining friendships, I would simply encourage you to make yourself available to someone who needs help. I'm convinced the best way to have friends is to be a friend.

Although blessed with sustaining friendships throughout this period of my life, I have to say that one of the hardest things I had to do was learn how to ask for help. Admitting I needed help was one of the most humbling aspects of my journey. As a minister, I was geared to help others. As an adult, I wanted to be self-sufficient. Thus, admitting that *I* was in need was no easy thing. In this respect, I am convinced we would do a better job of being church if we could be honest with each other instead of trying to project an "I have it all together" image.

ENCOURAGEMENT

Barnabas's role in Paul's call to be an apostle to the Gentiles is well known (see Acts 9:26-27). After an encounter with the risen Lord, Paul turned from being the church's persecutor to being a passionate proclaimer of the gospel. Still, many in the church in Jerusalem were skeptical and reluctant to extend fellowship. Barnabas, however, was the exception. Luke captures it beautifully: "and they were all afraid of [Paul], for they did not believe he was a disciple. But Barnabas..." (Acts 9:26b-27a, NRSV). But Barnabas! Something about Paul's experience rang true with Barnabas, and so he embraced Paul and took it upon himself to be Paul's advocate. He vouched for Paul, and from that point on, there was no question about his standing or his calling. Barnabas, "the son of encouragement," believed in Paul when no one else did and stood up for him.

As my sojourn in the wilderness dragged on, I wondered a lot about my future. Was I done? Did I have anything to offer? I desperately needed a Barnabas and the gift of encouragement.

Barnabas showed up for me in three different guises—not individuals but communities. Each community showed up for me at just the right time. Each one extended some much-needed encouragement, helping me regain both my self-confidence and my confidence in my gifts and calling.

I begin with First Baptist Church in Chattanooga. After a long search for church family, Ginny and I eventually became members there. The church was downtown and took its call to minister very seriously, as evidenced by its embrace of the homeless and the impoverished. The church also valued worship. The services were well designed and combined reverence and warmth in a delicious mixture, a tricky thing to pull off. Ginny and I fell in love with this church. We were at home there, and their welcoming embrace jump-started our healing.

Our pastor, Thomas Quisenberry, instinctively recognized our need for space and didn't flood our inbox with requests to serve on committees or take charge of a ministry effort. We needed the respite and were grateful for it. Over time, however, I think Thomas recognized that I needed to put my gifts to work again. Thus, he invited me to preach on two occasions. I gladly accepted those invitations and relished studying a text and crafting a message. On the Sundays I preached, I was aware that I was rusty and not quite in rhythm. Still, the congregation responded positively. More than one person said, "You've still got it!" Wow! What a boost! My gifts, though a bit stale, had not expired.

A second development followed shortly thereafter. In fall 2018, a church member sought me out and informed me that his Sunday school class needed a teacher. The New Perspectives class, he said, was composed of people of different ages from diverse backgrounds. He went on to say that the members were thoughtful and enjoyed exploring ideas. Surprised by my own interest, I agreed to take on the role. His description of this bunch was accurate! This was truly an atypical Sunday school class. When asked questions, they didn't answer the way they thought they were supposed to. Instead, they were honest and forthright. They genuinely cared for each other, and I witnessed their generous welcome of guests. For the better part of a year, I had the privilege of teaching this lively and lovely group (or getting out of their way as they taught each other!). We pursued a variety of topics, and I eagerly embraced the task of weekly preparation. Most important, they encouraged me by affirming my teaching ability. Their embrace left no doubt that they accepted and believed in me. Assuming this role was one more step for me on the way to a new future.

In these ways, First Baptist Church came and stood alongside me. Through their encouragement, I was able to take some baby steps on the way back to fulfilling my vocation.

Encouragement also came my way by means of a rich and powerful learning experience. In April 2018, I began my coursework at the Institute for Transformational Leadership at Georgetown University for training as an executive leadership coach. Being accepted into this program was a high honor. Out of a sizeable number of applicants, I was one of thirty-two chosen to participate. Cohort 53 was extraordinarily diverse. The participants came from wildly different backgrounds and cultural experiences. To illustrate the rich diversity of our group, I'll simply note the following: one of our members was Jewish and worked for AIPAC, while another was a devout Muslim from Riyadh, Saudi Arabia. As well, members of the cohort were tremendously accomplished in their respective fields. Nevertheless, the one thing I came to appreciate most about this group over time was that they were beautifully human. They were incredibly generous with affirmation.

To illustrate, as a part of our first session, we were divided into small groups. Each member of every small group had been given an assignment to complete before meeting at Georgetown. We had been asked to write a watershed story, one that captured a moment of personal growth, discovery, or transformation. The description of this assignment included these words: "The story is simple but is not necessarily an easy one to tell." I decided to take a risk and write about my decision to walk away from the ministry, not knowing how those who were not ministers and perhaps not engaged in any faith practice might hear it. At the very least, I thought their feedback might provide me a new vantage point from which to see and understand the way my life had unfolded.

If I remember correctly, I was the last of our group to share a story. The group listened intensely as I opened up about the events of the preceding years. When I finished, I took a deep breath and waited for their response. To my utter surprise, there was no awkward silence at all. Instead, each person responded by offering comments that conveyed their understanding and their affirmation. Imagine that! From a group of total strangers, I received an outpouring of encouragement.

Fast-forward from that event in April to our last session in October 2018. On one of our last days, we were asked to reconvene our initial small group (the first meeting in April was a one-off; after that we were divided into learning circles that subsequently met during each session). Our assignment was to offer observations about our perceptions of each other, particularly in terms of personal growth and development. In sum, this is what the group said to me: "You've changed! Something good has happened to you, and you are different." When I pressed them for specifics, they said, "You're more at peace. You project more confidence. You just seem lighter. You're better than you think you are." At one of the lowest points in my journey, when I was hobbled both physically and spiritually, a group of total strangers showered me with encouragement. I don't think I have ever had a richer experience of unconditional affirmation.

To the above I must add that my experience at Georgetown led to the formation of some strong and abiding friendships. Lots of good conversations happened in and around our sessions. We got deep quickly and found lots of common ground despite our wide-ranging diversity. Those friendships continue to this day, and they have been an ongoing source of encouragement. For the record, I have to give a huge shout-out to Sonya, Bill, Julie, Doug, Eric, Mary Beth, Tim, Mary, and Shana!

One last "Barnabas" community deserves mention. In August 2019, Tyler Engle, the chair of deacons at First Baptist Church in Erwin, Tennessee, inquired as to my availability to serve as their interim. I assured him of my availability and interest, and that led to an invitation to preach on an upcoming Sunday as a sort of "trial sermon." On August 25, Ginny and I drove up to Erwin for the day. The following week, Tyler called to inform me that I had been called to serve as their interim. I was terribly excited.

The circumstances facing this congregation were unusual. Prior to my call, the church had already had two interim pastors, and both served until circumstances prohibited their continued ministry. During these interims, the church had selected a pastor search team, and they had done much of the heavy lifting such a responsibility entails: developing cohesion, determining what qualities the next pastor should possess, creating a church profile, and finally getting into search mode. The search team had gone about their work diligently and were preparing to interview potential candidates. Unfortunately, their work was put on hold by two significant events. One of the team's beloved members died, and another had to undergo serious heart surgery. The team eventually got back to work, but no viable candidate emerged after a series of interviews. As a result, the search team and the congregation were discouraged. They had been nearly two years without a pastor and were beginning to wonder if they would ever find the right person.

In light of where the church had been and where it was at the moment, I determined that my number one task was to renew this church's hope. I wanted to prompt the church members to think seriously about their future. I sought to affirm their strengths and gifts. At every possible juncture, I encouraged them to take a good look at their community and discover where and how their gifts might make a difference. To their delighted annoyance, I reminded them over and over that there could be no growth without pain. Business as usual wouldn't cut it. This was my role as their interim, and I did it well.

The contributions I made to this congregation, however, were small in comparison to the gifts they gave me. Because they called me to serve as their interim, I was able once again to engage in the weekly round of preparing to preach and teach. Pastoral care needs within the church reawakened the deep satisfaction that comes from showing up for someone else. In this role, I once again enjoyed getting to know people, learning their stories, and asking them about their faith. In short, this church trusted me. It had been a long, long time since I had experienced that, and it felt really good! By trusting me at this pivotal moment in their life, this congregation encouraged me by letting me discover that I could still do this work and do it well. First Baptist Church of Erwin gave me a chance to prove myself. They were Barnabas to me, and I was able to take my first sure step on the way out of the wilderness.

CONCLUSION

Centuries ago, the psalmist, recounting the history of the Hebrew people, called attention to their rebellion against God while journeying through the wilderness. Despite what they had witnessed of God's deliverance and provision, they asked a plaintive question: "Can God spread a table in the wilderness?" (Psalm 78:19b, NRSV). Can God keep us alive in the middle of the desert?

My answer to that question is a hard-won "Yes!" The sustenance God offers may not show up on a table overloaded with everything we desire. Nor is the evidence of God's sustaining grace always visible in the moment. The way God provides may not always be to our liking. Nevertheless, God can keep us alive when the way is hard and barren. During my time in the wilderness, I heard the flutter of angels' wings. I discovered that God had often set a table for me, not always with what I wanted but always with what I needed. And that was enough to keep me alive.

QUESTIONS FOR REFLECTION

1. When you endured your own wilderness, what did you need most?

2. How have you been sustained during difficult periods?

3. What images of God's providence have been most helpful to you?

4. Have you ever been carried by others? If so, who were those people, and what gifts did they give you?

5. Describe the ways you've experienced God's providence. What elements stand out for you?

CHAPTER 5

LESSONS

> *Although he was a Son, he learned obedience through what he suffered; and having been made perfect, he became the source of eternal salvation for all who obey him . . . .*
> —Hebrews 4:8-9 (NRSV)

> What did you learn in school today?
> —Any parent to any child

One of my dearest friends, reflecting on the failure of his business, offered up this gem: "We only learn when we hurt." I think his observation is spot on. Real learning rarely takes place without some difficulty or discomfort. Only a prodigy can play the piano without lessons and tiresome practice. Mastery of math or a foreign language comes at the price of long hours of homework and tedious repetition. Farmers know that it's good for some plants to be stressed by a spell of dry heat; the absence of surface moisture prompts the roots to reach deeper into the soil. Character develops only when one adheres to deeply held values when it's not easy to do so. Life lessons are not gained in the abstract; instead, they are conveyed in real time and in the rough and tumble of daily life. We may not care to admit it, but there's a lot of truth in the statement: we only learn when we hurt.

This assumption underscores the writer's assertion in the book of Hebrews that Jesus learned obedience through his suffering. That statement may be a bit jarring since we tend to downplay or refuse to think too deeply about Jesus' full humanity. In fact, we hold so firmly to Jesus' divinity that it's hard for us to envisage Jesus ever struggling to do anything God asked him to do and to get it right. As a counterpoint, the writer of Hebrews stresses that obedience to God didn't come easily to Jesus. He had to work at it every day.

Thus, when Jesus was tempted in the wilderness, his struggle was real. The encounter between the Accuser and Jesus was no drill, and it certainly wasn't play-acting. Instead of calling Jesus' identity into question, the Adversary presented Jesus with seductive alternatives for living out his identity and pursuing his ministry. The stakes were high, and the possibility of failure crouched at the door. In their accounts, Matthew and Mark hint at the intensity of this struggle by noting that angels ministered to Jesus in the aftermath (see Matt 4:11; Mark 1:13). Remaining clear about his objectives and true to his identity in the face of the Adversary's challenges was hard work and holding fast to both left him exhausted and worn out. Jesus wasn't participating in a controlled experiment with a guaranteed outcome. Far from it! Jesus' temptations mattered for him and for us because he could have failed. From the outset, Jesus had to work hard to remain obedient to God.[43] His faithful obedience was very much a learned behavior.

I have learned a lot through my sojourn in the wilderness, and the lessons, though invaluable, have been hard won. The Teacher, however, has been with me throughout, and the wilderness has been my classroom. As I bring this account of my journey to a close, I'd like to pass along some of the lessons I've distilled from my experience.

FAITH

Just as it was for all my forebears in the faith, my sojourn in the wilderness, when boiled down to its most basic form, has been a test of faith. The experience sifted me and forced me to crawl under the house and inspect the foundation of my walk with God. Here's what I found.

"Just trust the Lord!" I heard this admonition countless times over the last several years of my experience. For the faithful, that is a "go-to" exhortation. Haven't we said this to people who are enduring hardship or facing complex decisions? Don't we encourage them to give such matters to God? Our earnest repetition of this bromide assumes that faith is the prescription for any problem. Just believe, trust, have faith, and all will be well.

While I wholeheartedly subscribe to the importance of trusting God, it is not as easy as it sounds. Believing in God's good purpose is extremely difficult when life is stuck in neutral. Remaining faithful to God becomes complicated when one has good reason to wonder if God really cares about individual people. Holding on to the promise of God's graciousness when frequent and fervent prayers yield only silence—well, that will frustrate the stoutest soul. In Karl Marlantes's novel *Matterhorn*, one character freely admits that Jesus could be "just one big fairy tale." Despite that, he tells his friends that every day he chooses to believe all over again anyway. He sums up the matter succinctly: "It ain't no easy thing."[44] No, it isn't.

Beyond such obstacles lies a practical matter. *How* exactly does one trust God? Is it simply a matter of praying and handing things over to God? Is it a one-off experience? "I gave it to God, and now it's all in God's hands." Or is it something that must be reaffirmed more often? My time in the wilderness has taught me that faith requires daily (and sometimes hourly!) dedication. Early in my seminary education, I came across this insight from one of my assigned readings:

> Not much security lives in faith; no security from a previous experience can cancel out the risk. A person has to keep believing. The salt can lose its savor. Every day one has to be born again. There is no built-in guarantee that carries over from a previous victory. Yesterday's faith will not necessarily support today's threats . . . .[45]

This assessment of what it means to believe rang true with me then, and it still does today—perhaps even more so! Trusting God is indeed a daily exercise. Trusting God requires persistence. Just because I managed to trust God yesterday does not mean that I will get it right today. Very few of us succeed in giving a matter of great importance to God once and for all. When we awaken each day, the stubborn and disturbing preoccupation awakens with us, and then and there we have to entrust it and the rest of our lives into God's hands.

Additionally, the admonition to "trust the Lord" carries with it the unspoken assumption that we'll be happy or at peace once we do. This understanding makes faith one-dimensional—like a flat and static cardboard cutout. Faith that matters, however, is multifaceted and densely textured. Faith speaks with many voices: gratitude, lament, questioning, hope, anger, and praise, to name a few. Many of these expressions spring from hard ground, but all of them grow from the same root. To speak in one manner and not another does not make a person's faith any less valid. As the previous chapters reveal, I employed a full repertoire in my conversations with the Almighty. And I realized I was in good company. The saints whose stories line the pages of Scripture could be both heroic *and* weak. At times, they had steel in their backbones; on other occasions, their spines turned to sand. They were all too human and subject to the ebb and flow of faith in daily life just as we are. Sometimes they stepped up; other times they shrank. *How they engaged God reflected where they were at a particular moment!* They spoke in a way that reflected life as it was and not necessarily as they hoped it would be. Regardless of the voice and manner in which we offer our prayers, all of them manifest our desire to bring the entirety of our life experience to God. Isn't that what trusting in God is all about?

Here's an additional discovery: God shows up in our wounds. The prophet Isaiah hinted at this unlikely and surprising truth as he sought to describe the Lord's Suffering Servant: "he was . . . a man of suffering and acquainted with infirmity" (Isa 53:3b, NRSV).[46] At least in North America, our understanding of faith has to some extent been corrupted by our society's obsession with success. Suffering and infirmity don't mesh well with the popular notion that God's sole purpose is to bless us and make us happy. As a result, we place a premium on testimonies that exhibit a strong "before and after" comparison. Before I met God, I was miserable, and my life was in shambles. After I met God, I was happy, fulfilled, and successful.[47] God looks good when our stories have happy endings or result in a cornucopia of blessing. Such things are truly a sign of the Lord's favor. Wounds and hurts? Not so much.

Paul upended the conventional thinking about faith as he responded to the "super apostles" with whom the church in Corinth had become infatuated. On the surface, they appeared to be everything Paul was not—powerful speakers with a compelling presence. They looked like what every believer in Corinth wanted to be. By comparison, Paul didn't fare well. He didn't always speak well. He wasn't flashy. Plus, Paul had some sort of infirmity that sapped his strength and vitality, something Paul called his "thorn in the flesh." To counter the message of the "super apostles," Paul put his weaknesses front and center (although he did engage in the "whatever they can do, I can do better" game by comparing his experiences with those who claimed to have special insight. See 2 Corinthians 11-12). He insisted that his thorn wasn't just something he was "stuck with" (pardon the pun!) but was instead how he experienced the full sufficiency of God's grace. Manifestations of power and ecstasy, Paul argued, weren't the only ways God showed up. Instead, the apostle insisted that God was deeply present in human weakness by means of this astonishing affirmation: "So, I will boast all the more gladly of my weaknesses, so that the power of Christ may dwell in me . . . for whenever I am weak, then I am strong" (2 Cor 12:9b, 10b, NRSV). In other words, our wounds, our weaknesses, and our struggles create more space for God to show up and meet us than our accomplishments and successes.[48]

I have also found this to be true. Life apart from ministry meant that all my usual identity markers and avenues for achievement were lost. For a long time, I didn't know who I was, and I ran into one roadblock after another trying to get my life on track. I was hurting in a lot of ways. As a result, however, I acquired a firsthand experience of God's grace in the midst of weakness. The previous chapter catalogs the ways in which I was sustained. I was carried by God's grace through my struggles in ways I never experienced during my seasons of strength.

Debie Thomas captures and summarizes this insight in her reflection on Jesus' appearance to Thomas that first Easter. She contends, rightly I think, that we misunderstand the nature of witness as evidenced by our preference for "battle scars over open wounds."[49] To illustrate, she calls attention to the appearance of Jesus' resurrected body:

> Jesus' resurrected body doesn't bear faded scars signaling a long-ago victory on a half-forgotten battlefield. They are fresh wounds, still raw enough to allow a doubting disciple to place his fingers into Jesus' side. Open wounds.
>
> I imagine Jesus winces when Thomas touches him. That pain—that openness—signals real life and engagement. Real presence. It speaks the very words Thomas hungers for the most: I am here. I don't float a few antiseptic feet above regular reality; I dwell in the hot, searing heart of things. Exactly where you dwell.
>
> Our wounds don't tell the whole story. But the stories they do tell are holy. If Jesus didn't fear the bloody and the broken, perhaps we don't need to fear them so much, either.[50]

Neither my wounds nor your wounds tell the whole story about who we are and the quality of our faith. Nevertheless, the stories penned by our wounds are incredibly holy and offer a more eloquent witness than those written in the ink of power and success.

PRAYER

The wilderness also imparted some new insights about the practice of prayer. As the preceding chapters make clear, I prayed virtually every day. Some days I felt circumstances closing in, and as a result, my prayers glowed with a white-hot intensity. Other days it was all I could do to try to drag my soul before God, and my prayers were predictably feeble and inarticulate. Still, however and whenever I prayed, the discipline disclosed some fresh understanding about myself and also the practice of prayer itself.

For example, I learned yet again that I am not a natural contemplative! By temperament, I crave activity, work, and stimulation. I do enjoy brief periods of silence and stillness, but not for long. When things get too quiet, my mind puts on its running shoes and heads off in all directions. Before I know it, I'm way off somewhere, and I've left God behind. In this regard, I found that I did my best praying while I was on the move. For example, whenever I drove, my car became my tabernacle. Driving somehow centered me, and my prayers flowed more easily. The same goes for walking. Walking calmed me and made it easier to open up my life to the Lord.

This experience brought home the oft-repeated truth that there is indeed no one way to pray. Although we can certainly try new ways of praying (and we should!), our best prayer practices emerge out of our uniqueness. The important thing is to find a practice best suited to who we are as individuals.

What about the content of our prayers? Although I prayed regularly and often, I caught myself recycling the same words and phrases and the same concerns over and over. This awareness surfaced memories of conversations with other people who droned on and on, repeating the same stuff every time we met. Conversations like that bored me to death! In that light, I figured my praying must have wearied God to no end. Bill Ireland again? Isn't there something else this guy can talk about?

As a result, I tried several things to spice up my prayer life. First, I turned to the words and imagery of Scripture as a way of framing my prayers. Whenever a word or phrase in a particular passage caught my attention, I figured there was a reason. So I lingered there and gave the words time to germinate. I waited to see what, if anything, would come up out of my spirit. Many times, this practice allowed me to phrase my prayers in a way that was truer to what was in me. It turned my praying from dull repetition to more active engagement with God.

I also relied on the prayers of others for inspiration.[51] The honesty, creativity, and insight offered by my fellow travelers put words to my inarticulate groaning. Time and again, their words nailed my experience at a particular moment and enabled me to bring it into God's light. Their prayers gave me clarity regarding my spiritual struggle and the courage to speak it in my own way. Moreover, reading the words of someone praying exactly what I was thinking, feeling, and sensing assured me that I was not alone—a wonderful gift in itself!

I tried to let what I observed during my walks inform my prayers.[52] Everyday stuff, from sparkling streams to traffic jams, can become grist for the prayer mill. News reports, conversations, and even the things that make us laugh until we cry prompt us to speak with God. Because God dwells fully in our midst in and through Jesus Christ, everything is a potential sanctuary.

To vary my prayers, I experimented by jettisoning many of the typical words in our prayer vocabulary: bless, strengthen, comfort, help, guide, and give. Praying without those words is hard! As a substitute, I played with visual imagery. For example, if one of my friends was undergoing treatment for cancer, instead of praying that he might be healed, I attempted to visualize the treatment invading the cancer cells and destroying them. Or if a colleague in ministry was enduring a hard season, I would imagine her laughing at something and see her face relax and her eyes brighten. Since I'm a talker by nature, I wasn't always comfortable with this practice, but it did stretch me and gave me a new way to engage with God.

Finally, when it comes to content, although Jesus taught that we ought "to pray always and not lose heart" (Luke 18:1, NRSV), repetitive prayer is not always fervent prayer. Repetition may, in fact, signal the need for reappraisal of a particular matter. For example, when my prayers about something lost steam and degenerated into word salad, I realized I had likely exhausted the concern. It was time to let it go and move on. Such occurrences made me aware that something had shifted within me. Whatever the concern was, it was finally in God's hands, and my verbal barrage in God's direction was no longer needed. I was also surprised to discover that repetitive prayer is often counterproductive. Praying about a matter over and over may be necessary at the outset of a crisis or unexpected twist of fate. The intensity of the situation requires it. Over time, however, plowing the same ground over and over cultivates dissatisfaction rather than peace. For example, I prayed *ad nauseum* about my employment situation. I finally reached a point where I realized that praying about it was feeding my anxiety instead of relieving it. At that point, I resolved to let it go. My need was no less critical, but the repetitive nature of my prayers made things worse instead of better.

No matter the manner or the content of our prayers, the object of prayer is to bring our entire lives before God. Deciding not to voice certain things to the Almighty because they are too delicate or our emotions are too raw makes us the arbiter of what matters to God. When we attempt to hide our rough edges from God, we only succeed in shielding ourselves from God's incalculable grace. If we can't pray our lives as they are, then what's the use?

INTERPRETING LIFE

As I write this chapter, the COVID-19 pandemic has forced all of us to retreat within our homes and restrict our contact with others. To keep boredom at bay, people have binge-watched TV shows, devoted much time and energy to long-postponed home projects, and worked tirelessly on their lawns and gardens. Postings on social media also suggested that many are passing the time and keeping their minds occupied by assembling large and complex jigsaw puzzles. I wasn't at all surprised by this last development. Putting a puzzle together is an apt metaphor for what we all attempt to do in our lives—assemble a jumble of pieces in such a way that they create a coherent picture. The pastime is certainly appropriate in the face of a pandemic that has forced people into isolation, wrecked the global economy, and made a trip to the grocery store a life-threatening event. How do we make sense of the upheaval generated by this outbreak? Solving a puzzle fits where we are at the moment.

Here's another take. Lewis Smedes, the longtime professor of theology and ethics at Fuller Theological Seminary, wrote the following in his book *Caring and Commitment*:

> We are all writing our stories; and each of us has to write his or her own . . . . The trick is to write a continuing story. A story with a plot that has a central character. Not a collection of unconnected episodes about a collection of unconnected characters.[53]

In sum, this book is my effort to put the puzzle pieces of my life together so that they add up to something meaningful. By writing this book, I'm trying to write the "continuing story" of my life. As such, it's an exercise common to all of us. After all, human beings are meaning makers. We want to connect the dots in such a way that the pieces of our lives make sense. We want to write a coherent narrative of our lives, a narrative that has a beginning, middle, and end. That's the goal to which we aspire.

But this exercise is complicated by the fact that circumstances are tricky. Things don't always add up. This doesn't always fit with that. There's often an odd piece left over. What we expect and what actually happens are often very different. The features on our mental map of life as it's supposed to be don't always correspond to the terrain of life as it is. Life is much more difficult to figure out, and the wilderness taught me some important lessons in this regard.

When it comes to interpreting life, *our initial conclusions are not always right*, and I learned this truth firsthand. Clearly, some of the doors I thought were wide open turned out to be shut tight. Where I thought I was headed was not where I wound up.

Looking back, I think I gravitated toward certain conclusions for a couple of reasons. Some of them made sense at the time. I took stock of my life and concluded, "Aha! This is where I'm headed! This is what my experience is about!" My initial conclusions made sense not only to me but also to others who knew me well. They thought I was on the right track and saw things unfolding as I did. When I added their perspective to mine, the weight of evidence and intuition pointed to an obvious destination. It was an easy reach. We can't all be wrong, can we?

One other unstable ingredient was in the mix: I was in a hurry to get on to what was next. My wife Ginny often remarked that the fact that I was born two weeks early set the pattern for my life: I was always in a hurry to get somewhere! I naturally assumed that after a brief time I would enter the next phase of work and ministry. So naturally I gravitated to any suggestion that promised a quick reset. I latched on to anything that held out the hope of "sooner rather than later." In this respect, I failed to take into account that something profound had happened to me, and I needed more time to heal than I knew. When it comes to interpreting life, the hardest thing any of us will ever do is give God time. That was true for me. I quickly learned that trying to force God to run on my schedule was an exercise in futility. It simply couldn't be done.

Interpreting life means we also live with the tension between *anticipation* and *discovery*. When we ponder a major decision, we inhabit a space bound on all sides by anticipation. We force our imagination to work overtime so we can plot all the variables and possible outcomes. We attempt to sketch out the potential consequences. And, once the decision is made, we are often hopeful that events will materialize according to our best plans. Such anticipation breeds excitement. We look forward to what will unfold, confident that whatever comes will match one of our detailed scenarios. I quickly learned that, despite my extensive preparation, decisions often go awry. When that happened, I had to move on to plan B, C, and sometimes D! What I anticipated did not come to fruition. While frustrating and maddening, this recurring reality forced me to recalibrate, start over, and keep going. And the only way I could keep going was to find something, anything, to look forward to. Having something to look forward to keeps hope alive.

While many of my initial hopes and plans were disappointed, I was able nevertheless to look back and *discover* that God had been at work for good in ways I had not anticipated. Although my choices had not turned out as I hoped or planned, God had still worked with my choices in ways I could not have imagined at the time. Mark's account of Jesus' casting out of a demon from the daughter of a Syrophoenician woman offers instructive commentary at just this point (see Mark 7:24-30). Although Jesus was initially reluctant to grant this woman's request (a troubling assertion in itself!), he eventually relented—but only after some lively and pointed conversation. Jesus admired her persistence and told her to return home, assuring her the demon had left her daughter. In conclusion, Mark states, "So she went home, *found* the child lying on the bed, and the demon gone" (Mark 7:30, NRSV; emphasis mine). The word Mark uses for "found" here is a form of the word *eureka*, popularly rendered as "I found it!" In other words, when this woman returned home, she discovered that God had been at work even though she had not been on hand to witness it. Eureka! Discovery!

I had this in common with the Syrophoenician woman. I discovered that God had been at work even though I had not witnessed that work firsthand. Instead, God had indeed been at work while I was on my way and even when my back was turned.

What we anticipate and what we actually discover may not always match up. Yet, when we lean hard into the idea that God does not leave us without a future, we can receive the strength to keep going. When what we hoped for doesn't materialize, we may discover that God has been up to something entirely unexpected, something we come upon later in our journey. Interpreting our lives requires that we keep faith in the future and remain open to discovering something good that we never saw coming.

As well, the challenge of interpreting our lives requires that we come to terms with the fact that *we always make decisions in light of what we know at the time.* No more and no less. We have no idea how our choices will play out.

As I approached the decision to leave the church in Dalton, I had serious conversations with my family and some trusted friends. Ginny and I reviewed our finances with our advisers. I sought input from my leadership coach and my spiritual director. We weighed our circumstances and concluded that staying was only postponing the inevitable for six months to a year. We believed then, and still believe now, that we made the right decision, but we had no idea things would play out as they have. We simply could not see that far into the future.

We could not envision all the variables or all the possibilities that might come to bear.

Until this point, I had prided myself on my ability to make good decisions. Of course, I had made my share of bad choices along the way, but none of those were of great consequence. This time, things were different. Despite our thorough planning, life fell in on us. Nothing we tried worked, and I beat myself up a lot, insisting time and again that "I should have known" or "should have seen" x, y, or z. The truth is, no one could have known or seen these things.

I quickly realized that playing the "what if?" game was a waste of time and energy. Second-guessing our decisions was equally fruitless. I learned that no amount of obsessive and detailed preparation can take into account all potential eventualities. I had to cut myself some slack and come to terms with the fact that, although some things had not gone as we had hoped, we still had a lot for which to be grateful. Again, it was in this moment when we felt so vulnerable and exposed that we realized how God's grace had carried us.

When it comes to making significant decisions, the best any of us can do is make our decisions and live with them—all the while trusting that God meets us on the other side of every choice we make.

POINT OF VIEW

In Harper Lee's classic novel, *To Kill a Mockingbird*, Atticus tells his daughter Scout that there's a "trick" to getting along with all kinds of people: "You never really understand a person until you consider things from his point of view—until you climb into his skin and walk around in it."[54] To put it differently, where we stand determines what we see. Where we stand determines what we understand. Making my way through the wilderness has altered my point of view. I now look at life from an entirely different vantage point.

To be candid, my growing-up years were quite sheltered and secure. My dad was an exceptional farmer and made a good living for our family. My mom saw to it that my sister and I never wanted for anything and were free to take advantage of all opportunities that captured our interest. Together, my parents provided an environment that was predictable, stable, and comfortable; I never encountered any dire life or death struggles that put my future in question. All in all, life had left me virtually untouched. I had a very limited understanding of how suddenly and drastically life can change.

That youthful ignorance began to change as I lived into my calling. I quickly learned that life is terribly fragile, often hanging by the barest of threads. People's lives can quite literally fall apart overnight. Much of ministry takes place at the margins where chaos, suffering, and death thrive. I had been with people in those extremes but always as a witness and never a full participant. Whenever people admitted me into the circle of their sadness and suffering, I was always a guest. No matter how much I cared, I was an observer, on the outside looking in. Although I had a "feel" for what others endured, I never fully comprehended the depth of their experience.

The last several years have changed much of that for me. Through the loss of my identity as a minister, I have struggled to know my place and purpose in this world. I have a better understanding for those who are worn out from trying to find a way and not being able to—through no fault of their own. Breaking my ankle in three places introduced me to what it's like to live with the kind of sharp, jabbing pain that can jolt one awake in the middle of the night. Adding to my discomfort was the fear that I might lose my foot. For about four months, I held my breath, hoping the pain would ease and I would be spared amputation. As a result of this injury and recovery, every time I see someone shuffling along on a walker or wearing a boot, I wince. I know something of how exhausting it can be to get in and out of a car, shop for groceries, or go to the bathroom.

Through an unbelievably long dry spell of unemployment, I have had to cope with a loss of dignity and an accompanying loss of confidence and self-worth. I know how hearing "no" over and over and over again can grind a person down. I know what it's like to be certain that I could do a job well yet never be given a chance. I no longer wonder why many simply give up. Through an onslaught of doubts and questions, I have walked in some of the darkest alleyways of faith. There have been many times when I wondered if trying to keep faith was worth it. Wouldn't it be simpler and easier just to leave God out of it instead of trying to reconcile events with my pesky sense of calling? Through long seasons of waiting, I have lived with uncertainty from dawn till dusk. The security I had known for most of my days simply vanished. These were entirely new experiences for me.

Although new, these experiences have shifted my point of view. I like to think that I have indeed climbed into the skin—at least a little—of those who have a hard time getting out of bed every day. I like to think that where I've been has made me a little more understanding, compassionate, and gracious. My wilderness experience has certainly made me better equipped to "consider things from another's point of view," and maybe for now, that's enough.

CONCLUSION

As I look back over my educational pilgrimage, I have to say that the best teachers I studied under were the most demanding. They set high standards and challenged me and their other students to live up to them. They didn't tolerate "just getting by," and so they made that outlook anathema to me. They asked a lot of me, which forced me to up my game. Because their way was hard, I sweated and labored and ground away at stuff until I got it. Because they were unyielding in their requirements, I was forced to do more than I thought I could at the time. The passage of time has revealed that they weren't being demanding just for the fun of it. Besides being passionate about what they taught, they were also passionate about fostering growth and development. They didn't just want me to learn something; they also wanted to *make me something*. I'm better for having been in their presence.

The wilderness has been a hard and demanding teacher. This experience has asked a lot of me, and I didn't always want to do the work. While I desperately wanted things to work out neatly and on my schedule, the wilderness had a different agenda. The last several years have been terribly disorienting and uncomfortable. Yes, I've learned a lot. More important, however, I think I'm better for having been in this class. All I know for sure is that God's grace has been sufficient in ways I have already experienced and in ways I have yet to discover. As I write these words, the way forward may finally be opening, and I may be about to emerge from the shadow of the wilderness. To quote the title from one of Maya Angelou's books, I "wouldn't take nothing for my journey now."[55] I wouldn't want to take this trip again, but I'm glad I did. I went there, and it was painful. It hurt, and I learned.

If I had been around to write one of the Gospels, I know for sure I would have included the story of Jesus' temptation. But I think I would have added a little something. Just as the Gospels tell us that God smiled on Jesus when he was baptized, I would have written that when Jesus was on his way out of the wilderness, God met him about halfway. Together, they walked the rest of the way, Jesus allowing God to bear some of his weight. Somewhere along the way, Jesus felt God grasp his shoulder a little more tightly, and even if he couldn't see God's face, he knew in that moment that God smiled and was very, very proud.

May it be so for every one of us who has to take the hard way through the wilderness. Amen.

QUESTIONS FOR REFLECTION

1. How true is the statement "we only learn when we hurt" for you? Do you agree or disagree? Why?

2. Identify some of the hard places you've traveled. What did those places teach you?

3. What disciplines have enriched your practice of prayer?

4. How would you describe your life? A series of disconnected episodes? A narrative with a beginning, middle, and end?

5. Recall a time when your first conclusion wasn't right. What did that experience teach you?

6. When and how did you discover that God was up to something when you weren't looking?

7. How have your hard moments shifted your perspective and changed your point of view?

EPILOGUE

> *We shall never cease from exploration*
> *And the end of all our exploring*
> *Will be to arrive where we started*
> *And know the place for the first time.*
> —T. S. Eliot, "Little Gidding,"
> *The Four Quartets*

The above excerpt from T. S. Eliot's *The Four Quartets* speaks to the hope that our struggles, no matter how difficult, will yield something meaningful. Whatever prompts us to leave the safety and security of our comfort zone, we venture out in faith, trusting that wherever our journey takes us, we will gain some new insight and understanding. Once we embrace the struggle and work our way through it, we circle back to where we began but as entirely different people. Whatever we endured as a result of our exploration has the potential to illumine the things that prompted our departure in the first place.

I can think of no better way to sum up my sojourn in the wilderness. My uneasiness with the way churches typically operated and some persistent questions about faith drove me away from ministry for a season. As I've noted, I didn't expect this hiatus to last as long as it did, nor did I expect it to be so challenging. Nevertheless, I have finally circled back to where

I started but as an entirely different (and hopefully better) person.

To come back to where I started means that I will once again have the opportunity and privilege of serving as a pastor. In late September 2020, I began serving as the pastor of the Norris Religious Fellowship, an inter-denominational church in Norris, Tennessee. This was an exciting and unexpected development. Throughout this book, I have chronicled my "on-again, off-again" thoughts about returning to ministry. There have been many instances where I concluded I was done with pastoral work and simply needed to turn my attention elsewhere. I have also had moments when I just *knew* that ministry was still my calling and my life's work, the one thing that best expressed my truest self. Something about this opportunity has felt genuinely right and satisfying from the get-go. I'm back where I started, and it feels like home.

Allow me to describe how this turn of events came about. In fall 2019, I joined Pinnacle Leadership Associates, a consulting group dedicated to "partnering with others to discover and pursue God's mission in the world." Early in 2020, our founder and leader, Mark Tidsworth, announced we had received a grant to work with the International Council of Community Churches and provide resources to their ministers and congregations. To prepare for my role in this venture, I went to the ICCC website to learn more about their identity and mission. As I scrolled through their site, I came across a listing of open ministry positions and discovered that the church at Norris was searching for a pastor. Since Norris wasn't far from where we lived, I thought, "Oh, what the heck! I don't have anything to lose." So, I applied, and in summer 2020, things took off and resulted in a call to become the church's pastor.

This development confirmed some of my conclusions about God's providence. Certainly, God worked *within* the possibilities brought about by our move to Knoxville, where Ginny had secured work as a hospice chaplain. Although some additional opportunities had presented themselves early in 2020, they never came to fruition. In hindsight, I believe I was once again "saved from" those things so I could accept this call. God's providence once again showed up in the form of sustaining grace. As I recounted earlier, the focus of my prayers began to shift late in 2019. I had grown weary of praying for work. Having exhausted my prayers in that vein, I was finally able to let go of that particular concern. As a result, I entered 2020 with the stubborn and persistent notion that something good was coming. I was inexplicably at peace even though we still faced some struggles. Looking back, I believe God was "in" the chain of events that began with a conversation with Mark Tidsworth about a potential place of service with Pinnacle. God had not forgotten me, and God certainly did all God could do given the particulars of our life situation.

Having said that, I by no means wish to leave the impression that the ending of my time in the wilderness possesses the same kind of "happily ever after" quality we find at the end of Job or in other fairy tales. Ministry is hard work, and I am certain there will be days when I wonder why I ever wanted to do this again. But my struggles have taught me a few things, and like Job, I am willing to risk it for the opportunity to once again be true to who I know God made me to be. I have discovered that my calling itself is the "open door, which no one is able to shut."

The Spirit is driving me again, but this time I am on my way out of the wilderness. Already the terrain is turning greener, and the clouds are lifting. The light is breaking through. Life *is* good, and I am on my way to something new.

I'll let you know how it goes.

ENDNOTES

1. Parker Palmer, *Let Your Life Speak* (San Francisco: Jossey-Bass, 2000), 3.

2. Eugene Peterson, *Working the Angles* (Grand Rapids: Eerdmans, 1987), 2.

3. Karl Marlantes, *What It Is Like to Go to War* (New York: Atlantic Monthly Press, 2011), E-edition location 1447.

4. Peter L. Steinke, *How Your Church Family Works* (Herndon, VA: Alban Institute, 2006), 12.

5. Lewis B. Smedes, *How Can It Be All Right When Everything Is All Wrong?* (San Francisco: Harper and Row, 1982), 91.

6. Dallas Willard, *The Divine Conspiracy* (San Francisco: Harper, 1988), 36–37 and 41–42.

7. For a thoughtful and in-depth treatment of this subject, I recommend Edwin H. Friedman, *A Failure of Nerve* (New York: Seabury Books, 2007), 83–88. Our pursuit of quick fixes is a reactive response to anxiety.

8. Richard Rohr, *Falling Upward* (San Francisco: Jossey-Bass, 2011).

9. Rohr, *Falling Upward*, 47.

10. William Bridges, *Managing Transitions*, 3rd ed. (Philadelphia: DeCapo, 2009), 8.

11. Bridges, *Managing Transitions*, 8.

12. *Herrens Veje*, 2017, season 2, episode 10.

13. As of this writing, that number is now above seventy.

14. Revelation 3:8a, NRSV.

15. *Herrens Veje*, 2017, season 1, episode 4.

16. Harry Emerson Fosdick, *The Meaning of Prayer* (Nashville: Abingdon, 1962), 78.

17. See Mark 3:28-30. According to Mark, Jesus identified the "unpardonable sin" as the inability to discern the difference between evil and good in response to his adversaries' assertion that he cast out evil spirits through the agency of Satan.

18. Terence E. Fretheim, *Creation Untamed* (Grand Rapids: Baker Academic, 2010) 11.

19. Fretheim, *Creation*, 53.

20. Romans 8:28. Paul's wording in this verse is open to multiple renderings, such as "all things work for good" or "God in all things works for good." The interpretation depends on where the reader puts the emphasis. I have chosen to stress that no arena is closed to God. God can work and work for good in the midst of anything. Nevertheless, human cooperation is vital.

21. See Clayton Sullivan, *Called to Preach, Condemned to Survive* (Macon, GA: Mercer University Press, 1985).

22. Jeremiah 20:7 (NABRE).

23. Barbara Brown Taylor, *Home by Another Way* (Cambridge, MA: Cowley Publications, 1999), 167.

24. J. Gerald Janzen, *At the Scent of Water: The Ground of Hope in the Book of Job* (Grand Rapids: Eerdmans, 2009), 102.

25. Janzen, *At the Scent of Water*, 101–104.

26. See Samuel E. Balentine, *Job* (Macon, GA: Smyth & Helwys, 2006), 627.

27. Tony and Jan Cartledge, *Job: Into the Fire, Out of the Ashes* (Macon, GA: Smyth & Helwys, 2007), 102.

28. See, for example, Norman C. Habel, *Job*, OTL (Philadelphia: Westminster, 1985), 557–74, and Balentine, *Job*, 683–92.

29. Cartledge, *Job*, 103.

30. In *Genesis*, Interpretation Series (Atlanta: John Knox, 1982), 288ff, author Walter Brueggemann titles the section of Genesis featuring the narrative about Joseph as "the hidden call of God." For the purposes of my story, I adapted his idea and chose to speak of God's "hidden hand."

31. I will address this idea more fully in chapter 4.

32. E. Frank Tupper, *A Scandalous Providence* (Macon, GA: Mercer University Press, 1995), 64.

33. Tupper, *A Scandalous Providence*, 80.

34. For this insight, I am indebted to Martin B. Copenhaver, "Risking a happy ending," *Christian Century* 111 (October 12, 1994): 923.

35. In Harold Kushner, *When All You've Ever Wanted Isn't Enough* (New York: Pocket Books, 1986), 82.

36. Available atfamilyfriendpoems.com/poem/the-invitation-by-oriah-mountain-dreamer.

37. The word is *diakonun*, from which we get our word "deacon." It is used in the New Testament to suggest someone raising a cloud of dust in the rush to serve someone at the table.

38. Tupper, *Scandalous Providence*, 280–305.

39. Tupper, *Scandalous Providence*, 286.

40. Irony of ironies, Ginny was the ER chaplain on call when I was brought in with my broken ankle!

41. For similar examples, see Mark's account of the healing of the woman with an issue of blood in 5:24-34 and the account of Jesus' conversation with the Syrophoenician woman in 7:24-30.

42. Available atfamilyfriendpoems.com/poem/alone-by-maya-angelou.

43. That Jesus' temptation continued to the end of his life is made clear in Matthew 26:38-44. Jesus was tempted by the passersby, the religious leaders, and the bandits, each urging Jesus to come down from the cross and save himself.

44. Karl Marlantes, *Matterhorn* (New York: Atlantic Monthly Press, 2010), 466.

45. Carlyle Marney, "The True Believer," in *The Struggle for Meaning*, ed. William Powell Tuck (Valley Forge, PA: Judson, 1971), 27.

46. The more familiar reading is "a man of sorrows."

47. For this insight, I am indebted to William H. Willimon, *The Gospel for the Person Who Has Everything* (Valley Forge, PA: Judson, 1978), 9–16.

48. Walter Brueggemann, in *Genesis*, Interpretation Series (Atlanta: John Knox, 1982), 271, makes a similar point when he observes that "Jacob is a cripple with a blessing. Israel must ponder how it is that blessings are given and at what cost."

49. Debie Thomas, "Open Wounds," *Christian Century* (April 22, 2020): 37.

50. Thomas, "Open Wounds," 37.

51. See, for example, Ted Loder, *My Heart in My Mouth* (Indian Trail, NC: Innisfree, 2000).

52. Please see my journal entries in chapter 3.

53. Lewis B. Smedes, *Caring and Commitment* (San Francisco: Harper and Row, 1988), 38.

54. Harper Lee, *To Kill a Mockingbird* (Philadelphia: J.B. Lippincott, 1960), 36.

55. Maya Angelou, *Wouldn't Take Nothing for My Journey Now* (New York: Random House, 1993).

"...the way forward may finally be opening, and I may be about to emerge from the shadow of the wilderness."

Made in the USA
Columbia, SC
04 May 2022